beyond
BLACK
and
WHITE

beyond
BLACK
and
WHITE

REFLECTIONS ON RACIAL RECONCILIATION

GEORGE A. YANCEY

Baker Books

A Division of Baker Book House Co
Grand Rapids, Michigan 49516

Published by Baker Books
a division of Baker Book House Company
P.O. Box 6287, Grand Rapids, MI 49516-6287

Printed in the United States of America

Library of Congress Cataloging-in-Publication Data
Yancey, George A., 1962–
    Beyond black and white : reflections on racial reconciliation /
George A. Yancey.
        p.   cm.
    ISBN 0-8010-5697-7 (pbk.)
    1. Racism—Religious aspects—Christianity. 2. Racism—United
States. 3. Christian life. I. Title.
BT734.2.Y36   1996
261.8′348′00973—dc20   96-11260

Unless otherwise indicated, Scripture quotations are from the New American Standard Bible, © the Lockman Foundation 1960, 1962, 1963, 1968, 1971, 1972, 1973, 1975, 1977.

Contents

96314

Part 3   The Narrow Path

Part 4   Where Do We Go from Here?

Preface

As I finish the writing of this manuscript, affirmative action is undergoing debate in our nation's courts, the million man march is still a topic of discussion, and proposed changes in our immigration laws are being called racist.

Issues concerning race never seem to go away in our society. We like to think that the Civil Rights legislation of the late '60s and early '70s ended the problem of racism in our nation. At one point in my life I believed it did. I wish that I had been right. But Civil Rights laws did not end racial strife, and now I can see that it is naive to believe that laws alone could ever do so. Just looking honestly at the racial mess in our country today confirms that.

The more I have thought about this issue, the more I realize that the moral presence of the church is essential in the battle against racism if racial peace is ever going to be possible in our time. I have always loved the church—by church I mean the body of Christ, not any particular church body or denomination—but I now stand as a loving critic of this church because of the way she has handled, or more accurately failed to handle, the dilemma of racism that we see in our society today. I desperately want to see the church begin to explore ways she can help resolve racial turmoil.

I cannot be silent nor do I have all of the answers. The purpose of this book is not to provide all the right answers but rather to provoke questions and dialogue. We have not honestly asked the hard questions of what it will take to bring the estranged races together. Therefore we have not had proper dialogue concerning the problem of racism. This dialogue may have begun in the secular world, but only to a limited extent. Devoid of any real spiritual insight, the secular discussion of such a deep moral issue must always suffer from some degree of sterilization, being unable to produce the real fruits of reconciliation. The church, however, has avoided this discussion to a great extent. By presenting some blunt truths concerning our current racial situation, it is my desire to provoke dialogue in our Christian congregations today.

My faith in Christ leads me to believe that it is only within his body that an honest assessment of the positions of both minorities and whites can be made. For this reason I have tried to write this book while looking at the racial situation from a majority perspective and a minority perspective simultaneously. This was not always easy to do and I fully expect to be criticized by both minorities and whites. In fact, if I have written this book properly, I will also receive criticism from the extremists, those on the edges of this discussion. Trying to engender reconciliation is a difficult thing and those of us who attempt it must expect to be misunderstood at times. The criticism may be justified but I hope it also means that this book has touched sore spots among a variety of players. Maybe it will be at those sore points that honest dialogue can develop concerning our current racial turmoil.

My manuscript received critique before it was even published. All of the critique was constructive to a variety of degrees. Brian Warren, my intimate friend and the best man at my wedding, has given me the most helpful commentary. His friendship and his insights have been important in helping me develop a deeper sensitivity to the position of white Christians. He has helped me to incorporate into this book ideas that I may never have thought of on my own. I am grateful to him in ways that I can never fully express.

I also deeply appreciate the support and respect my wife, Sherelyn, has given me. Through her, the Lord is teaching me essential lessons concerning reconciliation. She is an invaluable partner who shares my vision of reconciliation within the Christian church on a variety of fronts.

I would like to thank my family for helping shape me into the man that I am. I especially thank my grandfather, George M. Yancey, who provided me with the best possible role model anyone could ever hope for, and my mother, Rose Taylor, who has been instrumental in encouraging me not to accept my lot in life but to dare to strive for the best possible education. It is an attitude that I hope to model for many in the next generation.

Other friends I wish to thank for direct and indirect contributions to the ideas in this book include Keith and Renee Atkinson, Mareen Kelly, Karen Tichenor, Dan Davis, Tiffany Leonard, Todd Gage, Doug Price, Daniel Morris, as well as a host of others too numerous to mention.

Finally I offer the greatest recognition to the Ultimate Reconciler, our Lord Jesus Christ. Only he can provide the insight, love, and wisdom that we need if we are going to learn how to heal the wounds that many of us suffer. Heaven help us if we allow these wounds to continue to fester.

PART 1

---

the
HIDDEN SIN

Can you think of a sin about which pastors of evangelical churches do not preach? At one point in my life I would have said no. Some preacher always seemed to be hollering at me about sex or honesty or pride. Oh, I admit that some sins seemed to get more play than others. Pastors seemed more worried about my sleeping around than about middle-class individuals' cheating on their taxes. (If I were cynical I would think that it was because middle-class individuals gave more money to the church!)

Lately, however, I have come to realize that the sin pastors and the church neglect the most is racism. I was a Christian for ten years before I heard a Bible study or a sermon devoted to aspects of racism. And while some ministries, such as Promise Keepers, have finally begun to deal with this issue I still find the church mainly silent about it. We Christians have paid dear consequences for this silence; disrespect from society, racism in the church, and our inadvertent support of a segregated society are among these costs. To be frank, as a black Christian, I tend to pay more of these costs than do my white Christian brothers and sisters. But we all pay the price, in one form or another, nevertheless.

There is a need in the church to develop an understanding of the problem of racism so that we can develop a proper response. I fear that we have been so silent for so long that when we do deal with the issue, we do so out of ignorance. I do not claim to have all the answers. Sometimes I think that I have nothing but questions. But before we can find answers, we have to try to understand the questions. Even exploring the questions surrounding racism can be an acceptable beginning point.

It is time to develop a dialogue with each other in the church and to begin to confront the hidden sin. We may think that the racial issue was solved in the '60s; it wasn't. The darkness of racism still remains even though the form it has taken has changed. We Christians must shine the light on this darkness so that we can see what is really there. We must understand how the nature of this sin has changed. It is only after we have begun to understand how racism is affecting our society that we will find wisdom sufficient to begin to deal with it.

It's in Me

Let your light shine before men in such a way that they may see your good works, and glorify your Father who is in heaven.

Matthew 5:16

During my last year in Austin I lived in the northeastern part of the city in an interracial neighborhood. One day while I was watching the news, I heard that there had been a police shooting. While not an everyday occurrence, this was not unusual in Austin; however, my interest was piqued when I found out that it was in northeast Austin. The story really got my attention when the news reporter mentioned a street that was very close to where I lived. Then I listened intently to the details of the story.

It seemed that a man had been harassing a woman and had been driven off earlier by the police. He was told not to come back to that address. Unfortunately he did not listen and came back later that night. The woman called the police and when they showed up, the man produced what appeared to them to be a gun. The man was shot several times and killed. Afterward the police discovered that what they thought was a real gun was only a toy weapon.

As I listened to this story, there was one overwhelming thought in my mind: *I hope that guy was not black.* You see, if the man was black then I would wonder if racism was involved in the incident. Would the police have used such excessive force if the man had been white? Not only would I wonder if racism might have been a factor, but I would anticipate the various African American political and religious groups beginning to place the label of racism on the incident. This was a reasonable fear after seeing the damage that similar incidents had done to cities such as Los Angeles and Miami. The city of Austin would be faced with a whole new round of racial introspection, not all of which would be helpful to the process of reconciliation. Later I found out that the assailant was white and all of these fears were put aside.

Even as I was putting these fears aside, however, a new set of fears began to crop up in my mind. I began to think about my desire that a man who had been killed have a particular skin color. To put my dilemma in perspective I imagined someone like David Duke wishing the same sort of thing I had. What would you think if you knew Duke had heard of a police shooting and said, "Well, I hope they shot a black man"? Images of white robes and burning crosses would probably cross your mind. Was I any better? Isn't hoping that an individual who has been killed is not black roughly the same as hoping that he is white? In horror I began to examine myself. Was I as guilty of racism as Duke? Perhaps my racism was merely different in degree from Duke's but not in kind.

I began to try to find ways to justify my thinking. After all, we know that someone like Duke would make his statement out of disrespect for the personhood of blacks. My thought was in response to the potential problems an act of racism would bring to my city. Surely my motives were more pure than those of someone like Duke. This excuse did not satisfy me for long. It may be true that I was responding to the societal situation around me; however, the grand wizard of the Klan could say the same thing. We have all seen pictures of white children at Klan rallies. When they grow up, they are just living by the lessons that society has taught them. In their minds, they are as certain that the mixing of the races is problematic to society as I was that a surge of protests after a racial shooting would have been. In both circumstances we are reacting to fears caused by society and thus allowing the development of racism.

This brings out a very important point about racism. We live in a racist society. Racism is not found only way down South or in certain neighborhoods. Unfortunately the phenomenon of racism is part of what makes America what it is. It is in our history and our culture. I am not trying to sound like some sort of unpatriotic radical; I am merely telling the truth. We cannot change a reality until we are willing to acknowledge the presence of that reality. I have to admit that racism is as much a part of my subculture as it is part of David Duke's. Racism is in David Duke. It is in the skinheads. It is in the black nationalists. But more important, at least from my viewpoint, racism is in me. The society has taught me to be racist

14

and I have learned those lessons well. I cannot ignore the realities of racism in our society, so sometimes, in reaction, I act or think in racist ways. I want to think that racism is something that is only found in those groups or individuals that we tend to think of as bigots. But now I am forced to be honest. It is in me as well.

I must say that this is a sobering revelation. If I am forced to admit that at times I act and think in a racist manner toward whites, this revolutionizes the way I have been thinking about the problem of racism in our nation. It is not just their problem anymore; it is my problem as well. I can no longer just see myself as the victim of racism but I am forced to admit that I am one of the channels in society through which racism can flow. Then, if I do not make a concerted effort to be a part of the solution to racism, I will continue to be part of the problem.

If I am not free of racism, what does that mean about others in our society? I'm sure no one who knows me would think that I'm racist toward whites. When I was a child I was accused of being an oreo because I had white friends. My best friend in college was white. Many of my roommates were white. Most of the churches that I have attended have been white. I am married to a white woman. I am firmly committed to ending racism and am repulsed whenever I encounter it. Yet in spite of all of this, I have found that racism lives in me. I am forced to wonder that if *I* am not free of this sickness, who in our society is?

It would be wrong for me to judge anyone but myself. Even though I used him as an example, I cannot say with 100 percent assurance that Duke is a racist. If you are honest, isn't it possible that some of the racism of this society has crept into you? We hesitate admitting this possibility because we have been told that racism is so evil. But I am not an evil person who is trying to impose some sort of black superiority on this society. You are probably not an evil person either. Let's stop slinging emotionally charged words such as "bigot" or "redneck" and become real with each other. If there is even the slightest possibility that racism resides in your life, there may be something in these pages that will help you deal with this sickness. Maybe something I write will help you understand the confused young blacks who often riot out of racial frustration or the Hispanic you have tried to befriend who seems to distrust you. If you are a minority perhaps you will begin to understand why your white friend cannot see the obvious racism that so disturbs you.

Racism has affected us all and my desire is to help others find a way out of it. Maybe in helping you I will be able to help myself. Somehow I think that encouraging each other to heal is part of an interdependence that is essential to Christians who are serious about being members of the body of Christ. So I challenge you to read on and I pray that the healing may begin.

We Made It Up

> Racism is a man-made, man-enforced phenomenon. Nobody, not
> even the Southerner, is born a racist.
>
> Calvin Hernton
> *Sex and Racism in America*

What makes me a black man? Most people would say that it is
my skin color. I am fairly dark. But if that is the major criterion for being
a black man, then what about the African Americans whose skin is lighter
than that of many whites? What about whites whose skin is quite dark?
Skin color *can* identify a person as black but it's not always an accurate
indicator of race.

What about other physical features such as my lips and hair texture?
Once again, while these features are distinctively black for me, they are
not so in all blacks. Furthermore, physical characteristics can be altered.
Skin color can be darkened through tanning. A perm can give a white
person a "fro." And I am sure there is surgery that can give one fuller
lips. If a white man made these physical changes would we then consider
him black? I don't think so.

Maybe it is culture that is the defining feature of an African American.
I have a historical heritage that no white person can ever completely possess. But what about the black child who is raised in a white family? Or
the white friends I have met over the years who are, for lack of a better
term, "wanna-bes"? They often seem more in tune with current black
culture than I am.

I am a black man and that status has consequences for me in our society. However, our difficulty in defining why I am considered a black man
can help us realize an important truth concerning racial issues. This is the

fact that racial distinctiveness is not a natural phenomenon. The criteria that our society uses to categorize us in separate races are not derived through a logical study of nature.

If racial distinctions do not occur as a natural phenomenon then how did they develop? Part of the answer is the fact that this concept of race is what we sociologists call a "social construct." It is something that society has developed on its own apart from the natural reality that surrounds that society. In short, we made it up. Over time we decided that this group of people should be of one race and that another group of people should be of a different race. Then different levels of status were assigned to the different races. We developed rules of segregation to control the mixing of the races. Eventually we actually began to believe that this separation is part of the natural order of things. Some of us Christians may even believe that God ordered this separation. All the while we forget that this is something we have made up.

Here is another way to think about race as a social construct. How many races are there in the world? three? five? hundreds? Are Hispanics a unique race or are they a version of the white race? Are the Japanese a different race from the Chinese? Are the English a different race from the French? There are no objective answers to these questions. In different cultures and subcultures the answers change. Biologists tell us that there are no "pure races" anymore and that all of us have varying amounts of different "races" within our genealogy. So race is defined sociologically rather than biologically. We have taken for granted that people belong to different races when, in reality, we are only buying into the definitions that society has given us. The definitions of race will vary from culture to culture and they change over time in any given culture.

Let's look at how changing definitions of race operate over time. Take, for example, the attitude in our society toward black-white marriages. There is still significant support for laws that would forbid such marriages.[1] I believe that such an attitude provides a useful indicator of the still strained relations between blacks and whites in this nation. This attitude against intermarriage is not unique to the history of black-white relations. In early America, marriages between the Italians and Irish were strongly discouraged. Such couples faced many of the same type of sanctions that interracial couples still face. Today, however, Italians and Irish can intermarry and suffer far less social pressure. Though there may be more black-white marriages today than ever before, there is still a lot of pressure against such unions and they remain a tiny percentage of all marriages. We are still struggling with interracial marriages in today's society because we still see blacks and whites as very different. We see Irish and Italians, however, as groups of people with no significant distinctions. In a society where there is not a strong perception of race, interracial marriages are entered into as easily as white interethnic marriages are today in our society.

The whole concept of a racial identity, then, is something that is socially constructed. I am expected to identify with someone who has my skin color. Why? Is it because we share the same experience? It is true that in this society many blacks share similar experiences. Even though blacks now share the same land mass as other groups in America and thus we could share similar experiences with whites, Hispanics, Asians, and others—if the culture around us allowed that—forces both internal and external to African American culture impose a shared identity on us.

Why is skin color the feature used to group us? Probably because it's the most obvious, but any physical feature could be used. The fact that I identify with individuals with my same skin tone is due to an arbitrary social construction of race that really has no natural meaning.

Let's look at this another way. I believe that most of my identity comes from my relationship with Christ. That is a choice that I have made. I feel that I have more in common with a Christian, no matter what color his or her skin, than I do with anyone else. Yet I cannot deny that, all things being equal, I identify more with a black than with a white. Thus I have a strong identity as a Christian and a weaker but still significant identity as a black man. The first identity is one that I have chosen and that has been given to me by God. The other identity I had no choice about and it was artificially constructed for me by the society in which I live.

Why is it so important to realize that racial identity and the concept of race itself are social constructs? We need to remember that race is not a God-given concept. All the misery that has developed because of racial issues is not part of the Lord's plan but is something that we have caused ourselves. We made up the concept of race. Don't blame this on God. Don't blame him for racial strife.

Today there are neighborhoods where I cannot safely walk because of the social construction of race. The same is true for whites and all other races. We have individuals preaching hate based just on skin color and individuals who will not trust anyone who does not share their skin color. Racism is truly a human creation.

Racism is not unique to America but it is far from a universal norm. The concept of racial superiority is a relatively new one in world history. Even today there are nations where racial distinctives may be recognized, but that does not mean the races suffer from differential status.

I believe that America is not any more evil than any other society. We see societies where groups are segregated or hated because of religion, geographic location, or family heritage. We Americans have chosen to discriminate by race. It seems that part of the depravity of the human animal is this need to create enemies to hate.

Racism then may be a social construct of American society because it is one way to perpetuate the sickness of hatred that has invaded the human soul after Adam's fall. This construct is exactly the opposite of Paul's assertion that God is not a respecter of differences—the differences that we often use to create our scapegoats—of race/ethnicity (Jew or Gentile), of status (slave or free), or of sex (male or female). See Galatians 3:28–29.

While it may be frustrating to realize that the racial insanity that we experience in this nation is nothing but a social construction, there is also hope in this fact. If we have made up all of this, then we can change it. I do not want to sound naive. Such changes are going to be hard and painful. Some will have to recognize a painful historical past. Some will have to learn how to forget that past. Racial relationships will have to be renegotiated. Whites will have to give up power. Minorities will have to accept responsibilities. But there is hope that it can be done. The peace currently experienced between Italians and Irish may eventually be experienced between blacks and whites. The racial barriers that we have created may be harder to tear down than historical ethnic barriers, but what humans have created I am confident God can destroy.

3

Real Racism
or Guilt Trip?

> ... Why are there no Martin Luther Kings around today? I think one reason is that there are no black leaders willing to resist the seductions of racial power, or to make the sacrifices moral power requires. King understood that racial power subverts moral power, and he pushed the principles of fairness and equality rather than black power ...
>
> Shelby Steele
> *The Content of Our Character*

It was just another story in the news. A prominent black politician was being accused of misusing his funds. His main defense was that the charges were racially based. I shifted uncomfortably in my chair. Why was he not defending himself directly against the charges rather than using the racial issue as a diversion? I wish that I could express surprise at such a tactic. In truth, I am more surprised when a popular black figure does not use the charge of racism to malign his or her enemies. This tactic is not limited to liberal blacks either. Who can forget the "high tech lynching" line of Clarence Thomas?

This charge of racism is often used against white Americans who do not hold the proper political views concerning issues of race. I find this troubling because I know that there are white individuals who do not endorse racism but who may endorse political and social policies that do not benefit minorities. Do they deserve the same scorn and stigma that is given to individuals who act in openly racist ways? But I am not just concerned with the welfare of whites. I believe that minorities do not help themselves by painting every white individual who may oppose certain political policies that benefit minorities with the brush of "bigot." It is entirely possible for a person to question the fairness and validity of affirmative action without having a racially bigoted motive for doing so. If we truly care about issues of justice, then we will be extremely careful about stigmatizing another person with a label that may be unfair.

I fear that our accusations of racism are sometimes used to intimidate others into blindly accepting a particular political viewpoint. Honest debate demands that we give all people a chance to present their ideas so that we as a society can reach a solution that is based on respect instead of fear.

True racism is the degradation of others on the basis of race. It should not mean that one has to endorse the proper political philosophy to avoid the charge of bigot. Of course at the extreme political positions there are certain policies that are obviously racist, such as Jim Crow laws. We weaken the impact of the word, however, when we charge everyone who does not agree with us as being racist. If nearly every act is racist, then almost nothing is racist, because we have diluted what being racist means. When that happens, individuals who are true bigots begin to lose their fear of public censure. They are free to act out their racism because to be charged with racism no longer has any meaning. There is little or no threat of a stigma to hold them at bay. Hateful racists gain the opportunity to become lumped together with those who are "politically incorrect."

This is a travesty. Bigotry does exist. It is rooted in hatred and seeks to harm others because of their skin color. The word describing such activities must have meaning. Therefore we must reserve the charge of racism for those who truly devalue others on the basis of race. It must not be for those who, in good conscience, endorse policies that may be subtly detrimental to minorities.

It is the responsibility of minorities to educate and debate with such individuals to teach the minority perspective on these issues. And we can learn from them as well. It is only in this way that we can help produce the sort of heart change that is necessary to have an impact on this society. I cannot do this by making racist accusations to someone because I have a political disagreement with him but I can teach him by explaining why I as a black man can be harmed by certain political policies and why I value aggressively pursuing racial justice. I must then trust the Lord to prick the conscience of this person so that the needed internal change can begin.

This interaction does not always bring a "conversion to racial awareness," but I believe that it makes a person's heart more fertile to an inner change so that he or she may begin not only to verbally reject racism but also to be more aware of subtle racist actions and attitudes that he or she unknowingly possesses. Such individuals may learn to become concerned for the welfare of the races. It is my responsibility and my privilege to allow the Lord to use me as a vehicle to promote this sort of change, which will make my life easier and, more important, will enable my friend to become free of the racial traps that Satan often lays in our paths.

As minorities we must be careful not to allow ourselves to use race as an excuse for our failures. It is easy to assume that we have been denied opportunities because of the racial barriers that still exist in our society. It is often difficult to know when race has played a part and when it has not, but excusing our own personal shortcomings or mistakes by asserting that we have run into racism is dishonest to us and to those whom we accuse. When I suspect racism, I must make sure that it is true prejudice and that my charge is not just an excuse for my personal failure.

If we are honest, African Americans must admit that part of the problem in the black community today is directly attributable to our own failings as black men and women, not to white racism. I have a feeling that this is true for other minorities as well. Pulling down our communities are blacks who are committing crimes against blacks, black boys who are producing kids that they are not ready to raise, and black youth who are failing to take full advantage of the little educational opportunities that are offered them and who look to drugs instead. This is not to discount the fact that institutionalized racism has created a climate in which these problems are made worse. However, when one becomes too focused on the responsibilities of others, one's own shortcomings become even more debilitating.

I recently watched a talk show where two prominent black women stated that poor black women had no choice but to become single mothers because of the environment in which they are raised. How ridiculous! I was born into a poor community but I chose not to engage in a lifestyle that produced kids I could not take care of or that got me involved in drugs. So while the choices of poor minority women are definitely fewer than those of wealthy white women, they still have choices. Laying the blame for wrong choices completely in the hands of the white establishment does no one any good.

Once as a kid I wanted to become part of a white peer group that was pretty popular. I became friends with one of the guys in the group but I was unsure as to whether I could win over the other members. So I used my friend by telling him that I did not think that the others would accept me because I was black. I didn't know that they wouldn't accept me, but I was pretty sure that if I made the accusation, my friend would try extra hard to get me into the group. I soon realized that what I had really done was cheat myself and my new friends. I cheated my new friends of the chance to accept me as I was without any unusual pressure from me. I cheated myself of the challenge of winning my friends over on the basis of my own personality instead of through racial intimidation. I used my race to keep me from examining myself and honestly dealing with real problems of character that I may have had. This is what Shelby Steele calls a "race-holder."[1]

I fear that we have become too adept at playing the guilt game. We African Americans have become quite good at making whites feel guilty. Shelby Steele notes that often African Americans use guilt so that they may seem innocent.[2] In doing so, blacks are able to gain power in society. Indeed, this tactic often gains us some governmental program as well as the status of a special-interest group. But this does not erase the fact that we have some internal problems that we must deal with in our communities. In fact we often reduce the race question to one of power, rather than one of morality. Steele notes that we concentrate more on how we African Americans may prove our innocence than on owning up to our responsibility. In the end, all this does is make whites more defensive and anxious to prove their innocence.[3] Thus the race conflict is exacerbated. Each side strives to hide its guilt so that each race may be seen as the victim. True innocence does not need to sound its own horn. Jesus proved that.

Minorities must realize that we have the responsibility to rebuild our families. We have the responsibility to rebuild our morals and values. Whites did not take away the values that held us together. We have given those values up.

Those of us who have succeeded in this society must strive to give something back to the community that we left. We must take the incentive to create our role in this culture, not looking to anyone to give us this role. The government cannot do these things for us. When we look to outside forces to do what we are responsible for doing, we ask too much of them and too little of ourselves.

When we believe the lie that we cannot accomplish anything without the help of whites, we give up the ability to empower ourselves. In a sense we lose our free will because we think that we are helpless to change anything unless we can extort help from whites. We forget about our own abilities and that we have the responsibility to make the most of the opportunities that are given to us, even while we work to bring about true justice. So in seeking to manipulate whites with racist accusations, we entrap ourselves into a parasitic dependency on those same whites we have just stigmatized.

Martin Luther King offered us a way out of this conflict. Rather than attempting to heap guilt on whites, he attempted to reveal the sin within society. Rather than striving to overcome whites, he strove to bring healing to them. He sought reconciliation rather than retribution. It was when the Civil Rights movement chose to concentrate on aspects such as black power that it lost the high moral ground. It attempted to gain power through taking power. King advocated gaining power through giving love. He recognized the harm that white racism had done but he also recognized the duty of African Americans to make the most out of any opportunity that was given.[4] There would be no unwarranted guilt trips, only the true attempt to bring justice to an unjust world. Therefore neither black nor white would gain advantage through a power play but all would learn to love each other.

This is the way true reconciliation may eventually take place as the races learn how to live with each other in love instead of fear. We minorities must even give up the right to feel the justifiable anger for the historic and contemporary wrongs we have suffered at the hands of a white society. Only in forgiveness will we truly lose the shackles of hatred so that we can replace them with the bonds of love. I think it will only be then that we will be able to avoid guilt trips and gain the powerful spiritual weapons that are necessary to combat the racism that still exists in our society.

4

Modern Racism

A century and a quarter after slavery, white America continues to ask of its black citizens an extra patience and perseverance that whites have never required of themselves. So the question for white Americans is essentially moral: is it right to impose on members of an entire race a lesser start in life, and then to expect from them a degree of resolution that has never been demanded from your own race?

Andrew Hacker
Two Nations

White supremacist ideology is no longer fashionable in our society. No one, except skinheads and Nazis, wants to be called a racist today. Thus we consistently find in the polls a high percentage of Americans who reject any notion that whites are superior to any other minority in ability and in value.

For the sake of simplicity let's call the attitude that whites are naturally superior to other races "redneck" racism. I am not trying to offend anyone. Many well-educated city slickers are redneck racists. It has nothing to do with where you live. Redneck racism is present when a business executive refuses to promote a Mexican American because "their kind" could never do such a difficult job. It's redneck racism when an African American is not allowed into a country club because of the unspoken assumption that blacks "cannot handle high class." Redneck racism is no respecter of class, location, or city size.

Quite simply the redneck racist believes that whites are superior to other races. Since this is the case, it is fair that whites are given extra privileges in society. Whites dominate society because they have the natural abilities to run society while other races lack these abilities. In fact the only reason that other races are able to compete on an even basis with whites is because they have been given an unfair advantage by measures such as affirmative action or Civil Rights law. The natural order of things is white rule.

Usually when whites think about racism, they are thinking about redneck racism. This is useful since it allows them to escape the responsibility of dealing with racism in our society. They know that redneck racists are out there but not too many of them. And they know that they are not redneck racists, so it is not their problem.

As a teaching assistant one summer I had the opportunity to sit in an introduction to sociology class while the instructor ran a film on the Ku Klux Klan. It documented well the movements of the modern Klan. I observed the reactions of the white students who surrounded me. From dozens of conversations that I have had with other whites I could guess what was on the students' minds. It was something like this: *Look at those idiots up there. Thank God I am not like them.* They left the class with their current racial attitudes essentially unchallenged. They believed that they had no real problem concerning racial issues and indeed such racism was no longer as prevalent as it once was.

As Christians, should we be surprised by such a reaction? It is natural for humans to run away from responsibility for their actions and attitudes. Our failure to accept responsibility makes it difficult for us to be repentant before the Lord. It is little wonder that our Lord admonishes that the way to him is narrow (Matt. 7:13–14). Few are even willing to admit that they need the path much less go down it.

If we are going to be honest about racial relations, we must look at how racism may manifest itself, other than in the redneck variety. "Modern racism" is one way.[1] Unlike redneck racism, modern racism does not assert any kind of superiority of whites. Indeed it claims to be as much a defender of egalitarian principles as any other philosophy in society.

Individuals who hold the views of modern racism would not admit to being racist. Indeed they are not racist by the way *they* define racism. For the modern racist, racism is defined as adhering to the redneck values of stereotypes, segregation, and open discrimination. Modern racists abhor any expression of these. Like the students in the sociology class they tend to believe that such actions are few and far between.

The ideology of modern racism states that racial discrimination is a thing of the past. In modern America there is an even playing field. Racial minorities can compete in the marketplace as well as whites, and therefore, any measures that aid minorities are seen as unfair since they give racial minorities an unwarranted advantage. When racial minorities push for changes, it is seen as unfair and undeserved. Any advantages given to minorities are unjust.

Therefore modern racism is able to justify resentment against racial minorities because minorities are unfairly gaining what they have through the power of a "special-interest group" rather than on merit. Modern racists question the justice of everything from jobs programs to minority scholarships. Modern racists may have several racial minority personal friends. They respect them as individuals yet are distrustful of minorities as a group.

Modern racism is largely responsible for the racial tensions of our day. Whites believe that nonwhites have made unfair gains in society, and nonwhites believe that whites are still working to keep them out of the places of power.

Have minorities made unfair gains in American society? Undoubtedly racial minorities have made gains in political power and in social acceptance. Modern racism does not deny the validity of such gains. But there is resentment when it comes to the possible economic gains of minority groups. It is believed that racial minorities may be gaining an unfair economic advantage, but the statistics don't bear this out. For example, the average black male made 54 cents for every dollar that his white counterpart made in 1950. In 1989 this figure was 56 cents.[2] The unemployment ratio of blacks and other races to whites in 1948 was 1.7 to 1. That means for every 1 percent of the white population who was unemployed there were 1.7 percent of blacks and other races who were unemployed. In 1990 this ratio was 2.4 to 1, or 2.4 percent of the blacks were unemployed for every 1 percent white unemployed.[3] Finally, in 1959 for every 1 percent of the white population that lived below the poverty level 3.2 percent of African Americans lived below the poverty line. In 1990 this figure was 3 percent African Americans for every 1 percent of the white population that lived below the poverty line.[4] On almost every economic indicator, African Americans have not improved their economic position relative to white Americans in the past thirty to forty years. The same tends to hold true for Hispanics, although reliable statistics on economic indicators for Hispanics are hard to find before the 1970s.

In the '50s and '60s it was clear why racial minorities did not do as well as whites. Racism was overtly oppressive. If modern racists are correct, however, and today we live in a fair society, then economic differences

28

between the races should be decreasing. Indeed there is evidence that women's income relative to that of men has been rising as American society has dealt with sexism. Yet we have not seen such changes when it comes to racial minorities. The assertion of modern racism that racial minorities have made unfair gains in recent years doesn't hold up when we examine economic statistics.

The discrimination of our history did not go away just because we passed Civil Rights laws. Rather, it seems plausible that racism has been institutionalized into our society in mechanisms that are not inherently racist but that operate in such a way as to maintain the advantage that whites have over racial minorities. Institutional discrimination may be operating in subtle, yet effective, ways to help maintain the current status quo.

Modern racism tends to give explanations for the continuing economic disparity between racial minorities and whites by focusing on factors other than racism. Yet most of the explanations are affected by the subordinate position that minorities occupy in our society. For example, some individuals who hold to tenets of modern racism argue that it is the instability of minority families that has contributed to their subordinate position in society rather than any form of discrimination. However, poor families tend to be less stable than middle-class families no matter what race one examines.

It is true that poor minority families, particularly African Americans, are less stable than poor white families and that this instability may play a role in their misfortunes. It is imperative that African Americans search for ways in which our family structure can be strengthened. We cannot dismiss racial explanations of this phenomenon, however. Even when the family is intact, the average black family is poorer than the average white family. And white single-parent families are better off financially than black single-parent families. Therefore family structure cannot be the only reason why blacks are not doing as well as whites in our society. One cannot totally discount the importance of race as a factor of minority poverty. When advocates of modern racism hold exclusively to nonracial explanations for minority poverty, they ignore factors having to do with race, such as segregation, inferior schools, and biased criminal justice system, that have been shown to impact living standards in our society.

The problem with the ideology of modern racism is not that it is entirely wrong. Indeed there are viable nonracial reasons for racial disparity and in many ways the lot of minorities has improved over the past thirty years. The problem with modern racism is that its basic assumption—that racism no longer exists—is false. But this assumption leads adherents to believe that all attempts to bring equality to the races today are unfair and actually racist against whites. Ultimately, solutions that lead to the reconciliation of the races are going to have to deal with racial and nonracial factors. Modern racism is willing to deal only with the latter at the expense of the former.

I suspect that if blacks possessed the dominant position in society, we would be doing the same thing: attempting to maintain our historic advantage with our current system. The presence of organizations such as the Nation of Islam testifies to the fact that racism is not just a disease afflicting whites.

What should be the Christian response to modern racism? Should I be able to count on my white Christian brothers and sisters to look after my interests and not their own if I am victimized by society? The state of racial relations today presents white Christians with a powerful challenge. They must be willing to see the fallacies in modern racism and to challenge it, even though such challenges may negatively affect them.

My gamble is that from my brothers and sisters in Christ I can hope for an honest and sometimes painful look at racism. Racism is not just a problem for minorities; it affects us all. It is a problem that all races must work together to overcome. Success through working together. That seems like something our marvelous Lord would plan.

5

Why?

Certainly evil is to be expected in a fallen world. What is not expected is for a holy people to accept it.

Charles Colson
Who Speaks for God?

Why does racism exist? For me as a sociologist this is an important question to ask about American society, which has made decisions about the value of being identified with a certain race and has enforced these values through socialization and sanctions. Why do humans continually pick out an arbitrary set of characteristics so that we can discriminate against each other?

Why does racism exist? As a human being I confront this horror in our society and wonder why. It seems very plausible that all individuals are equal. It makes no sense to hate a person because of something he or she has no control over and something as superficial as skin color. Human beings are unique on this earth. Shouldn't we be looking for ways to bond with each other rather than ways to tear each other apart? Racism can only divide us. It cannot enhance the survivability of the human race; it can only threaten it. How can we allow such a dysfunctional phenomenon to continue?

Why does racism exist? For me as a black man this question has profound implications. At one point in my life I felt that I could merely ignore the racist attitudes of others and perform to the best of my ability. In this way I could prove myself as an individual, apart from race. However, I now know that I will never be accepted by certain individuals or in certain situations no matter what kind of person I am. My race will always stand in my way. Those people will always see my race before they see me.

31

Why does racism exist? As a Christian I must face what surely must be an affront to God. Are not all Christians part of the same body in Christ? If this is so, then how can the body war against itself? When the biological body wars against itself, we call it cancer. For a body to war against itself is to guarantee the eventual death of that body. The Christian body does not have a soldier to waste as we fight the forces of this world. If we destroy each other and reject each other on the basis of race, we will bring sickness and perhaps eventually death to the body. We must learn what it means to build bridges rather than barriers.

I struggle with the question of why racism continues to exist. It seems so simple to me. We should all just forget about the distractions that racism produces and concentrate on loving each other. But the baggage we carry into our racial encounters seems to be too firmly attached for us to let go. We find ourselves holding tightly to old beliefs and old fears.

I honestly believe that most of us want to stop being concerned about race. It would be nice to forget about it. It's so tiring trying to figure out whether we have offended someone of another race or wondering if an individual of another race is going to accept us. Yet we Americans seem powerless to let it go. Why?

Perhaps part of the answer to my question lies in other countries that seem to have little or no racism. We may look at these other societies and admire their apparent lack of racism. Often, however, what appears to be tolerance on the surface is not what it seems.

A student of mine once remarked that when he was in military service in Europe he did not feel discrimination because of his race but because he was an American. It seems that all American soldiers feel this discrimination, regardless of race. Apparently even racially tolerant societies have a problem with tolerance in general.

Herein may lie my answer. The United States, like all societies that I know, needs a scapegoat. Scapegoats are useful. Without a scapegoat we would be forced to find in ourselves the reasons for our problems and shortcomings. But with a scapegoat we can blame at least part of our problems on another. People in all societies seem to need other people or groups to blame for their problems. This leads to intolerance and racism.

Racism may be an American problem but intolerance is a human problem. We do not need race to find individuals to hate. Look at the Croatians and Serbs. They are the same race and they are killing each other. The real question then is how do we as humans come to the point where we can stop looking for reasons to hate each other and instead work to find ways to love each other? When intolerance disappears, racism will wither away.

Despite what one might think, I have not found the answer to intolerance within the progressive, enlightened academic culture in which I find myself. It's true that academics tend to be more tolerant than most Americans toward certain lifestyles. I readily admit that we Christians can learn some lessons from them in the acceptance of other cultures. And academics are tolerant toward ideas and behaviors that do not threaten their basic assumptions about life. Groups and movements that threaten their belief system, however, often experience the wrath of the "tolerant" academic community. Other writers have done a good job of documenting this intolerance.[1]

If we are going to build a society where hatred, not merely racism, becomes a thing of the past, then we must find a way to love those whose ideas and actions may seem threatening. Education, despite its claims, does not seem to be the way. Many in academia will claim that they are not focusing blame on a scapegoat when they attack their critics but are instead accurately assessing a source of injustice—namely the groups that have threatened their "scientific" beliefs about reality. The temptation is always to exaggerate the influence of those who disagree with us when things are going badly and to minimize them when things are going well. In that way we can take credit for our successes, but not our failures. Even though others are able to influence our own personal well-being, I believe that ultimately whether we develop a complete life or not rests with internal instead of external forces.

Somehow we must find a way to accept our own shortcomings without having to find a scapegoat to blame for them. This is exactly where our trust in Christ can save us. If it means nothing else, being a Christian must mean that I have given up searching for my own standard and I have accepted God's standard. But in doing so, I must recognize that I have fallen short of that standard. To be a Christian is to accept the fact that I cannot meet God's standard and that I must trust that Christ will accept me even though I continue to fail him. I am, therefore, free to admit my shortcomings and failures since to become a Christian is to already admit that I am a failure.

If this is all true, then true Christians do not need scapegoats. Instead we need to feel the freedom to repent of our sins and to be reconciled with those whom we have harmed and with those who have harmed us.

As a Christian I am free from the need to blame others. I can freely admit that I am a fallen creature and that I am responsible for much of the misery that I see in my life. Unfortunately many Christians do not see repentance as freedom and continue to try to find excuses for their shortcomings. Therefore they become no better off than their worldly friends and feel a need to find scapegoats. And the hatred goes on, with Christians making things worse instead of better.

In my experience I have found only two types of individuals who do not seem to seek after scapegoats. The first type are individuals who have such low self-esteem that they are unable to place blame on others. However, such individuals are usually so self-deprecating that they are dangerous to themselves. This is not the model that we should seek to imitate. It would only replace hatred of others with self-hatred.

Unfortunately the second type seem to be far fewer in number. They are Christians who have learned to so completely die to self that there is no longer any reason to seek to blame others. They are not self-deprecating because they realize that God thought them of such worth that he sent his Son to die for them. They are not looking to blame blacks, liberals, Jews, atheists, or any other group for the problems around them. Rather, while they may acknowledge the sinful patterns of others, they seek to love them in ways that may produce real change in the lives of their enemies. It is in the increase of such Christians that racism and all forms of hatred can eventually be eradicated. Such godly men and women are too few among us in the church, and we all must begin to develop such qualities in ourselves and in our fellow brothers and sisters in Christ.

The challenge for those in the church then is to be willing to repent of our sins of intolerance and racism. As we do this and die to self, we can be free to be the reconcilers that the Lord wants us to be. Perhaps the question is not why racism still exists but why we Christians have not been obedient to our Lord. Why do we not live out what we believe? By doing so we can be the leaders who can drag this nation, kicking and screaming if necessary, through the painful process of reconciliation. Are we willing to confront the deeply rooted sins that we and our ancestors have brought to this nation? Are we willing to stop finding blame in others and take personal responsibility for the racial mess we live in? If we fail to do so now, I am afraid that thirty years from now another young man may be forced to once again ask, "Why?"

6

Can a Black Be Racist?

> I have one great fear in my heart, that one day when they are turned
> to loving they will find that we have turned to hating.
>
> Alan Paton
> *Cry, the Beloved Country*

It no longer surprises me. The topic of the group discussion was "what is racism?" I knew that it was just a matter of time before someone said it: "Only whites can be racist since they own the powerful institutions within society." Here we go again. Both white and black students in the discussion continued to defend the proposition that in America only whites can truly be racist due to the disproportionate power that they have in society. It is a belief shared by Sister Souljah and Minister Farrakhan. It does not sit well with me.

The "Right to Hate"

I have my own personal theory as to why some individuals subscribe to this belief. I think that whites who subscribe to this theory are basically trying to do blacks a favor. They recognize that many of the advantages that they have received are due to the fact that they live in a white-dominated society. So in an effort to make at least partial repayment to the minorities that have been cheated, they give blacks the right to hate in ways that they feel would be morally wrong for whites.

This may be noble, but it's not doing blacks a favor. Hatred is wrong no matter who does the hating. It's true that, for the most part, blacks have more reasons to hate whites than vice versa, due to historical and institutional discrimination. But we cannot justify hating a white person or a black person. Our Lord does not allow us to. All are equal in his eyes. Blacks must develop enough love for white individuals to help them overcome their racism. Whites must develop enough love for blacks to help them overcome their bitterness. This can only be accomplished when both parties are honest about difficult feelings that have developed between them.

I have also theorized that blacks often endorse the white-only racism theory to create more power for themselves in society. If it is okay for blacks to display a racist attitude but not whites, then blacks may gain a weapon to use that whites do not have. When one party is forced to seek the approval of the other, but the need is not reciprocal, then the former party is at a disadvantage as far as developing a fair relationship. Blacks sometimes use this ploy to gain power.

I wish that I could say that we Christians are generally innocent of using any such ploy to gain power. Unfortunately many times I have observed Christians use politics, status, or money to empower Christians, without any real concern as to whether their cause is just. Christians get angry if other groups in society threaten our security, but we seem to have little concern if groups in our society perpetuate injustice for those who have less power. The problem with this is that every time I read the Bible it seems that Jesus gets a whole lot more upset at the abuse of the downtrodden than any trespasses of his own rights. If we are serious about imitating him then we'd better put more energy into bringing justice to those victimized by our society and less energy into protecting ourselves. Maybe then we can find the faith to trust our Lord to be our protector.

As a Christian I am no longer free to examine the racial situation as a power struggle between the races. To do that is to adopt an "us versus them" mentality. It means that I must plan on how I am to win this struggle. I must seek power for my group, even if taking that power is at the expense of others. This is not what the Bible teaches. The Bible forces me to adopt a belief that all Christians are of one body. If I harm white Christians in an effort to gain equality, I am wrong. I do believe that whites will have to make sacrifices to bring about a more fair system in this nation, but these sacrifices must come from love, not fear. They should make such sacrifices because they believe it is right to do so and they desire to do what is right. I must put aside any weapons of retaliation and search for methods that unite rather than further divide the races.

I question whether this right to hate can ever be truly beneficial to blacks. What happens when an individual keeps anger bottled up inside?

Psychologists tell us that depression is often anger turned inward.[1] The ultimate paradox is that I may do to myself what the racist is unable to do: destroy my spirit. I can become a hateful man and eaten up with anger. I am always sad when I meet an angry minority who practically devotes his or her life to hating whites because of some racist incident or incidents in the past. Is this the sort of power that we want to reserve for ourselves? It is important that we do not allow hatred to dominate us—for our sake as much as for the sake of those who become the objects of our hatred. So I reject the right to hate that some African Americans are seeking.

While I disagree with the premise that only whites can be racists, I do think there is a kernel of truth here. Racism in America has been institutionalized, has become so much our way of life, that white Americans have disproportionately benefited. It's a fact that institutional racism was developed and has been perpetuated by whites. While members of other races can and do exhibit personal racism, most do not have the power of whites in our society. Only whites in this country possess power over the various minorities. It is in this way that white racism differs from the racism of minorities and thus should be more carefully monitored. Attempts to correct this imbalance of power are in order and are not in themselves necessarily racist.

If we want to end racism in this country we must be prepared to battle both institutional and personal racism. Too often individuals who espouse the theory of a white-only racism see only the societal racism of this nation. They struggle to end this form of racism through governmental and social assistance but fail to recognize the need to touch hearts. On the other hand some individuals are quick to point out that all races have personal racism but they ignore the evidence of institutional racism. They see programs that seek to end institutional racism as racist because they deal only with white racism.

We must call all individuals to combat personal racism within themselves. We must recognize that the races are still not equal within this societal structure and that this must be corrected, even though it will cost the majority race the historic advantages they have enjoyed.

The Power of Love

Of course the real solution to racism will combat both institutional and personal racism. The more we allow ourselves to know each other the easier it will be to learn how to love each other. That means that I as

37

a black man must not only love whites, but I must allow them to know me so that they may learn how to love me. When we model the sort of love that Christ has commanded us to have, then I believe we will see even the most racist of individuals begin to rethink their ways. I am not talking about a wishy-washy love that is afraid to stand for anything. I mean a love that will confront evil wherever it finds it and that will challenge the sin of the world. I am talking about a love that gladly bears the suffering of that sin so that it may be revealed and dealt with. It is not easy to love others that way. Often minorities would rather retreat into our own ethnic group so that we may gain power and use that power to accomplish our ends. This is a shortcut to power but it gives us little or no legitimacy. The tougher way is to go out from our own racial subculture and to confront the evil of racism in our world face-to-face, to dare racism to continue while we shame it with our love. This is the essence of Martin Luther King's nonviolent method. We need to think about how we can recapture it.

Not only will this sort of love shoot holes through the personal racism that so often bedevils us, but I believe it will be an important factor in the ending of institutional racism. Whites who develop true friendships with minorities often find themselves reformulating their ideas about some of the racist structures that we find in society. Perhaps this is why I have found that many college students are so open to examining racial issues; they are forced to live in an interracial environment and have developed friendships with minorities.

It takes courage to do the humbling thing of going out and befriending individuals whom we do not understand. It's probably easier to demonstrate our anger in spectacular ways, such as through protests and confrontations. Such methods often give us a temporary rush of power but may push away those whom we want to enlighten. There is a time for confrontation, but it is the mundane work of building relationships that will eventually be of invaluable assistance in ending the racial tension that we suffer in this country. You cannot easily oppress that which you love.

In our natural state hatred often overcomes love. If I reflect on what happened in the life of my ancestors and how even today I am often devalued because of the color of my skin, it becomes frightfully easy to become angry. But when we rely on Christ's love to lead us, then the love we thought was impossible can become a part of our new nature.

As a black Christian, I must become more concerned for the state of all individuals around me than for the black race alone. I must fight for love for the human race.

Asking if a black can be racist is the wrong question to ask. It seems designed to relieve me of responsibility and point fingers at others. Rather than engaging in tactics that will justify my shortcomings, I must look for Jesus' solution. This is Jesus' solution to the problem of racism: You should love your neighbor as yourself (see Luke 10:27).

7

I'm Not Racist but . . .

> . . . most Americans are people of good will. Most of us really do
> like other people, even those who are not like us. We prefer that
> they not be too close, however. We like those people in the abstract,
> not in the concrete.
>
> William Pannell
> *The Coming Race Wars?*

Modern racism is a philosophy that allows whites to express resentment over the attempts of others to improve the lives of minorities. Another type of racism in America is what sociologists call aversive racism. Aversive racism is similar to modern racism in that it rejects the doctrine of white superiority. It also freely accepts the overt integration of minorities within society. Therefore it is acceptable for blacks to move into a white neighborhood or for whites to work beside Mexicans. Yet individuals who adhere to this type of racism do have antiblack or anti-Mexican bias. This is evident when the individuals justify their prejudice on nonracial grounds.

For example, an aversive racist may tell you that he or she totally accepts the fact that his or her child goes to a school that has blacks in it. On a survey this person will indicate that members of all races should be allowed to attend any school that they want to attend. This person would not remove his or her child from a school that had a number of minorities. However, this person will turn around and oppose minorities on an issue such as busing. The aversive racist will say that this opposition has nothing to do with race. Rather, he or she will cite the importance of neighborhood schools or the inconvenience of having children bused. And of course these are reasonable arguments that one may make against busing. But if we could see into the heart of the aversive racist, we would see that what is truly shaping this person's attitude about busing is not the inconvenience (it is amazing how many of these same individuals will send their children to a private school at a great cost and inconvenience in order to avoid this "inconvenience"), but it is a hidden bias against minorities. Data from some sociological studies seem to indicate that part of the opposition to programs such as busing or affirmative action is at least in part due to aversive racism.

The modern racist might try to offer intellectual reasoning that justifies a resentment toward programs that attempt to aid minorities, but the aversive racist is more emotional. He doesn't try to explain his subjective and impulsive bias against minorities, but he also doesn't admit that he *is* biased.

What are the differences between modern racism and aversive racism? In many ways they are two sides of the same coin. Modern racism is cognitively based. It is an ideology that on the surface seems to argue against racism but in the long run supports the current inequities in the system. Aversive racism is emotionally based. Like modern racism, aversive racism denies traditional racism. But the aversive racist still has emotional biases against individuals of other races. It is possible that one individual may be both a modern and an aversive racist. In fact, I suspect that the two go hand in hand.

Many minorities are aware of modern and aversive racism. Some say they would rather deal with the old-fashioned bigot because they know where they stand. It is often difficult to know what ideals members of the majority hold. When they are insensitive to our needs and advocate measures that may be harmful to us, we are forced to question their motives. Often these people are politically conservative and though not all political conservatives are racists, the views of many are not sensitive to the needs of minorities. For example, opposition to issues such as affirmative action is not always based on racism. An individual may legitimately feel that affirmative action programs are an inefficient way to correct the problems of race within society. It is too simple to measure racial attitudes merely by political affiliation, but we cannot ignore how aversive racism has infiltrated our society. No lasting solution to racism is going to be complete without dealing with the subtle ways that racism is manifested. Those who are concerned must examine their attitudes. If they have been accused of being "politically incorrect," perhaps they should not just shrug it off. Some of what is called being politically correct is simply being sensitive to the needs and feelings of those who are different from us. Is that something Jesus would frown on?

41

I do not for a minute think that following politically correct rules is the solution to aversive racism. Often an individual will abide by the correct rules just to avoid being judged a bigot, yet negative feelings remain within. That is part of the insidious nature of aversive racism. We do not always recognize aversive racism in our actions. We can do just enough "good" actions so that we feel we can justify negative actions or attitudes against individuals of other races. If we do not recognize and deal with this hidden sin it will fester and grow within us ready to strike at any time.

To recognize the possibility of our own aversive racism, we must be willing to do some self-assessment. Admitting that the problem may exist makes it possible to deal with it. There are tools that may aid in this assessment. For example, Dr. Tony Evans has developed a self-test for whites and blacks to evaluate whether racism lies within their hearts.[1] For blacks there are questions concerning whether they stereotype other blacks as "Uncle Toms," whether they would admit that African Americans have problems unique to their communities that cannot be blamed on racism, whether they would promote a more qualified white over a black, and whether they demean whites merely because they are white.

For whites there are questions concerning whether they perceive black men as lazy, dangerous, or violent; whether they would be opposed to their children dating African Americans; whether they would live in a majority African American community; and whether they confront friends who tell racial jokes.

Such instruments can be useful but only if we have opened our hearts to the possibility of our own aversive racism. If we hold on to the belief that we cannot possibly have this type of racism, then all the self-assessment instruments in the world will not be of any use to us.

As Christians we know that the natural tendency of the human heart is to hide our sins away and to think ourselves better than what we really are. These tendencies are barriers to honest self-appraisal and virtually guarantee the continued existence of aversive racism where it exists. As with any other sin we must come to the Lord in humbleness to allow him to examine us and we must be ready to repent of the sin he reveals to us. Without the willingness to repent we have as much chance of overcoming our sin as an alcoholic has of overcoming his or her addiction when he or she won't admit to having a problem. The solution then must begin where the problem began—in our hearts.

8

Institutional Discrimination

We have inherited choices that were originally made specifically in the interest of racial separation.

Spencer Perkins and Chris Rice
More than Equals

Racism is more than personal prejudice. Institutional discrimination operates in our society and impacts the life of every minority. We can define institutional discrimination as the discrimination that is incorporated into the social structures and norms of our society. This phenomenon is made possible by historical injustices. These injustices build a society in which discrimination is a natural part of that society, whether those who live in the society are racist or not. An examination of how this process may have developed and how it affects us may help us understand the nature of our present situation. An institution that will serve as a useful example of the effects of historical racism is our educational system.

Residential Segregation

Ever since times of slavery, African Americans have been residentially segregated from white Americans. In the South this was accomplished through the development of Jim Crow segregation laws. Starting around 1915 employment opportunities began to lure blacks to the North. There the norms of residential segregation produced inner-city ghettos, which served to keep the races separate. Today we still see this pattern. There is no large city in the United States where blacks and whites share equally the same neighborhood. In fact in most cities one can guess with tremendous accuracy the race of a person by knowing his or her address. Much of what is called institutional racism or discrimination operates as a result of this type of segregation.

This historic residential segregation has effected our educational system. As blacks have moved into neighborhoods, whites have fled those neighborhoods. Modern studies show that when a neighborhood becomes 8 percent black, white residents leave that neighborhood and no new whites move in; thus the neighborhood soon becomes all black.[1] This phenomenon, known as "white flight," has served to produce inferior schools for African Americans. As whites move out of the inner-city neighborhood, they abandon the inner-city schools. Often these schools were the topflight schools of their time. Ron Sider gives an excellent example of what happens after this:

> In the early 1950s Northeast High School in Philadelphia was famous for its superb academic standards and its brilliant, long-standing athletic triumphs. The second oldest school in the city, Northeast had excellent teachers and a great tradition. And it was almost entirely white. Then in the midfifties, the neighborhood began to change. Black people moved in. Whites began to flee in droves to the Greater Northeast, a new all-white section of Philadelphia. Quite naturally, a new high school became necessary much further out in this developing, overwhelmingly white area.
>
> When the excellent new school was completed in 1957, the new school took along the name, Northeast High School, with its fond memories and traditions and many connotations of academic excellence and athletic triumph. The inner city school was renamed Edison High. The new school took all the academic and athletic trophies and awards, school colors and songs, powerful alumni and all the money in the treasury. Worst of all, the teachers were given the option of transferring to new Northeast High. Two-thirds of them did.
>
> The black students who now attended Edison High had an old, rapidly deteriorating building, frequent substitute teachers and no tradition. Nor did the intervening years bring many better teachers or adequate teaching materials. The academic record since 1957 has been terrible. In fact Edison High has only one claim to uniqueness. . . . More students from Edison High died in Vietnam than from any other high school in the United States! . . . Many would deny any personal responsibility. . . . Do we sin when we participate in evil social systems and societal structures that unfairly benefit some and harm others?[2]

Sider's description of what happened at Edison High points to the fact that neglect of the training and the education of African Americans sets up a vicious cycle that is difficult to break. Blacks are unable to get ahead because they lack the training and the skills to achieve success. Society sees that blacks lag behind whites when it comes to achievement in the economic world. It assumes that blacks are not able to learn as effectively as whites and therefore cannot be as successful as whites. Rather than acknowledging the differential opportunities that face the two groups, many assume that blacks simply do not have the abilities or motivation to achieve. Because blacks are assumed to be inferior, there is little incentive to improve the educational facilities of blacks and perhaps even less incentive to give them an equal chance at a decent job. The achievement of blacks remains low, and the cycle continues.

It is reasonable to assume that, like blacks, other minorities have a distinctive history that has played a role in creating inequalities by which our present system continues to operate. In fact my own personal experience was not in an African American school but one that had a high percentage of Hispanics.

My school had a wonderful vocational program. Every year we built an entire house from scratch. In the city there were a couple of high schools that put more emphasis on preparing their students for college. For many of the individuals in my school, college was not considered to be an option. They were trained to be part of the blue-collar workforce.

If all individuals in the city had access to any city high school this could have been a rather good system. But a student could go to a school in another district only if he or she could establish some sort of special hardship that only that school could help. In other words, where you lived determined whether or not you went to a school that specialized in bricklaying or one that could prepare you for college. The Hispanics of my district tended to be channeled into the blue-collar workforce, while the white students in the other districts were trained for college.

Many students were pleased with the vocational training they received at school. If that was where their natural interests and skills lay, they were probably grateful for the chance to get a head start on their vocation. However, if those interests and skills were better suited for a professional career, they and the community were cheated by their being channeled away from a chance to fulfill their potential. I might add that many white students who were better suited for vocational rather than academic training were also cheated by this system.

Such a subtle system of discrimination allows many of the beneficiaries of that system to be ignorant of the advantages they enjoy. They do not realize that extra academic resources have been made available to them at the expense of others. Therefore when they drive by the construction site and observe the many Hispanics in it, they can come to the conclusion that Hispanics tend to work such jobs because they do not have the motivation and the aptitude to achieve at higher status jobs.

White Preference

Sider, in his book *Rich Christians in an Age of Hunger,* points to the neglect of Christians to consider the ramifications of their actions. By vacating integrated neighborhoods we resegregate society and our school system. We may gain in property value and even send our kids to better schools. The desire for these things is not wrong, but often we have no concern for the students left behind. We are not willing to financially help those who are trapped in the inner city since we are safe in the suburbs. Our generation may not have created the institutions that made residential segregation possible, but we do not seem to be in a hurry to challenge those institutions.

Segregated neighborhoods seem to play an important role in establishing institutionalized discrimination and apparently they reflect the desires of whites. Indications are that blacks desire integrated neighborhoods more than do whites.[3] Since the number of blacks in this nation is about 12 to 13 percent of the total population, proportional integration can never take place. That is, we will never have an equal number of blacks and whites in all neighborhoods. Neighborhoods suffer when they are earmarked as black. Property values decrease, leaving less tax revenue for neighborhood schools. Obtaining credit becomes more difficult for individuals who live in such neighborhoods. There may be fewer businesses serving these neighborhoods because many businessmen do not want to operate in "the bad part of town."

There are no discriminatory laws that support white flight. The resegregation merely happens because whites perceive that there are too many blacks in a certain neighborhood so they move out. The African Americans who are left in the neighborhood suffer the consequences. If they have the resources, they may try to establish themselves in another integrated neighborhood and hope that blacks stay below the 8 percent "tipping point." This shows how blacks, as well as other minorities, face discrimination not only due to overt racism, but also due to a subtle rejection that the ideology of modern racism rarely acknowledges.

Segregated schools are often related to segregated neighborhoods. Institutions that unfairly disadvantage racial minorities will never be abolished until there is deliberate acknowledgment that these institutions exist. Deliberate steps must then be taken to remove the barriers set up by these institutions.

For example, if we are not careful, private Christian schools may become not only havens from secularism but also from exposure of our children to the children of different races and ethnicities. We should acknowledge that in the '60s some of the original intentions of private Christian schools were to provide a way for whites to avoid sending their kids to newly integrated schools. Today this may not be the case, but it's easy to see that many of our modern private Christian schools are highly segregated. Therefore children are not exposed to different races, and understanding between the races is thwarted. This is not just a disadvantage to the minority student, but also to the white student who does not learn how to interact with the different racial minorities that will inhabit his or her life after graduation. A careful rethinking of the purpose of Christian schools may be in order if we are to avoid inadvertently using them to support a segregationist system. We must think about how we can design Christian schools that promote integration rather than perpetuate racism in society. The challenge is not an easy one but it is one we must take up.

Our education system is a good example of institutional racism. It is a vicious cycle. Residential segregation leads to inferior schools that lead to inferior jobs that lead back to inferior neighborhoods. Residential segregation devalues the houses that blacks tend to live in and works against them when they apply for loans. Because of historic segregation, this cycle is built into our society and it will likely continue until we intentionally break the pattern.

There are other examples of institutional discrimination that must eventually be challenged as well. For example, seniority laws benefit whites more than blacks because of the historic advantage that whites have enjoyed. Blacks have not been in well-paying jobs for very long. And insurance costs for black businesses are often higher than for their white counterparts because of the areas where they operate.

These issues are difficult to deal with because the discrimination is often not deliberate. Seniority laws and insurance standards have been set without being related to discrimination. Yet these rules work against minorities, and we must carefully rethink how to apply them. Some will criticize changes in these measures as being racist against whites. I do not agree with such assessments but I do acknowledge that changes may often have to be race conscious. Racial preference, however, is already built into our society. Until we confront the historic demons that haunt us and find solutions to the institutional injustices in our society, individual, personal racial tolerance will never completely undo all of the wrongs that minorities face in our culture.

9

The Requirements of Discrimination

> Equality has long been an authentic American dream. Whether it can ever be reality in the sphere of racial and ethnic relations remains to be seen.
>
> Joe R. Feagin
> *Racial and Ethnic Relations*

I do not believe in reverse discrimination. I've already said that blacks and other minorities can be guilty of racism—there are plenty of blacks who are bitter and hateful toward whites—but I believe this is personal racism and not reverse discrimination. Personal racism is hateful acts committed by an individual against another of a different race. A person of any race can be a racist in this sense. Discrimination is something that the society does to a group of people. It is different from racism, which is something that one individual does to another individual.

Okay, what about those minorities who get a job or into colleges with lower test scores than whites? Is that not reverse discrimination, society discriminating against whites? Those who accept this as discrimination fail to understand the full nature of discrimination. Understanding this concept may prove useful in helping us figure out how to handle race relations in our society.

A System of Discrimination

Discrimination is not just an isolated incident but it is an entire system that works to the detriment of an entire group of people. Real discrimination happens in a cultural and historical context. There has been wide-

49

spread (obvious and subtle) discrimination in this country by whites against minorities in most institutions, housing, education, and the legal system. It has occurred over centuries of time. It is not just an isolated event that can be explained away or seen as an anomaly. When understood in this way, one can see that a single example of lower test scores by itself is not the same as the widespread institutionalized discrimination minorities have experienced in our country.

Let's look at this in another way. Assume for a moment that I walk into an auto dealership and buy a car. My new car costs me about one thousand dollars more than it would cost a white man. Is this situation different from the one in which a white student is denied admission to college while a black individual with a lower score is admitted? Both of these situations involve differential treatment because of race. There are important diferences, however.

First, it is important to look at why I paid more money for my car. The auto salesman probably stereotyped me as a less sophisticated buyer than a white person would be. This may have led to an attitude that made him less willing to bargain with me since he believed I was not smart enough to realize I was being duped. Now, it is possible that if I were a really sharp buyer, I would be able to work the price down to what a white man would pay. But if the image is that blacks don't know how to bargain, then clearly I'm going to have a harder job getting a fair price than would a white man. In fact, data indicate that African Americans pay more for their cars than whites.[1]

Second, it is important to note that this exchange takes place in light of a given history that blacks and whites share. From slavery to share-croppers to higher prices on cars, African Americans have historically been victimized by whites. This historic victimization has kept blacks from having the same expectations of success that many whites have and so has kept blacks from competing in certain arenas of our culture. Studies have indicated that African Americans believe they have less self-efficacy than whites.[2] Self-efficacy is the belief that one has the power to make things happen, to be successful in society. The centuries of oppression that African Americans have faced may mean that it will take centuries for blacks to develop self-efficacy to the same level that whites possess it. Some believe that blacks have been victimized to such an extent that this development may never take place. So my exchange with the car salesman was determined in part by the fact that society has historically denied me the opportunity to learn how to fend for myself. Institutional discrimination like this takes place in a historical context and reinforces old lessons, which make the continuation of such discrimination possible.

For the whites who weren't hired or admitted to colleges even though their test scores were better than those of blacks who were admitted, there is no historical context of being made to feel inferior that these experiences would reinforce. They can write off the experience as "unusual." African Americans do not have that luxury. We are forced to see a racist incident as just another incident in the long line of cultural discrimination that we have faced. It is not that white Americans do not suffer from the consequences of racist incidents. Clearly they do. However, because society has traditionally supported European Americans, most whites are able to suffer through the discrimination without its having long-term effects and hindering their ability to function in society.

Minorities are not always free from such repercussions. We are forced to wonder even when incidents are supposedly racially neutral whether there is evidence of discrimination. When denied a job or grade by an individual of a different race, the question of discrimination must come into play. As more minorities obtain positions of power within our society, whites may eventually wonder the same thing. However, currently it is still the overwhelming norm for a white individual to be in power.

This leads to a third crucial reason why there is a difference between my car incident and the incidents concerning test scores. Even if we assume that everything is at an even level in today's society, which is a big assumption, one cannot deny that whites still occupy the positions of power. Thus although there may be isolated incidents of racism that white individuals may suffer at the hands of minorities, clearly it is racial minorities who are at the mercy of the dominant white group in this nation. Our nation still experiences racial tension, and racial minorities often suffer from a pattern of prejudice while whites merely have to learn how to deal with isolated incidents that may occasionally arise. Institutional discrimination, then, is that which happens consistently over a wide range of events in one's life rather than merely being isolated to a few incidents.

I happen to be the first member of my family to obtain a college education. I am not the first because I am the first smart person in my family. I am the first because my family has suffered the pains of traditional discrimination. This discrimination penalized my ancestors directly and me indirectly, since I had no one in my family to guide me to success in college nor did my family have the finances to support me.

I realize that there are white families who have never had a member graduate from college. Racial discrimination is not the only reason that a family may not have anyone who is college educated. However, it is clear that for that white family racism was not the main factor stopping them from obtaining a college education. It may have been a variety of other factors: poverty, poor schooling, a lack of an academic tradition. But we know that racism was not the key factor.

It is clear that because of historical racism whites still occupy a higher place in our society than do minorities. Whites who live today have either directly or indirectly benefited from the fact that their ancestors had an advantage over my ancestors. Therefore, because of their heritage, white Americans are richer and better educated than minority Americans. This is not to say that there are not poor, illiterate whites in today's society. These families are poor and illiterate, however, despite—not because of—historic racial discrimination. Prejudice and racism against European Americans should not be taken lightly. I would be the last to argue that abusing whites is justified even though whites have historically abused other races. But the prejudice that whites sometimes feel today does not begin to equal the overpowering traditions of racism that not only have placed me at a starting point in society below most whites, but that continue to disadvantage me.

What would it take for there to be reverse discrimination? Whites would have to suffer oppression for hundreds of years and be constantly demeaned, being told that they are not fully human. This could happen through genocide, as it did for Native Americans; through slavery, as for African Americans; through oppression, as for Hispanics; or through a type of concentration camp, as for Japanese Americans.

For reverse discrimination to take place, whites would have to fight for decades for simple human rights. They would have to endure insults from those who lead their country. They would have to be locked out of positions of power, having others, who do not have concern for them, make decisions that greatly affect their lives. This has not happened and is not going to happen to whites in this nation. So whites do not face institutional discrimination as minorities have faced and continue to face.

The Current Task

I believe that many of the factors that have supported legal racial discrimination in this country have been addressed and outlawed. We have a long way to go but we have come a long way. I believe that the relationship between racial minorities and whites has changed to such an extent that blacks will never be completely subservient to whites again. This is good not just for racial minorities, but also for whites who can have true fellowship with us.

This change in relationship brings about its own set of problems. Now racial minorities and white Americans have to renegotiate their relationship. Perhaps part of the source of the racial tensions that we see in America today is this renegotiation. Many minorities, if they are honest, would probably express a desire to pay back whites for the misery that has been done to them. Some whites may fear this and thus work to keep minorities from gaining the power to exact their vengeance. Likewise many whites, if honest, would admit that they desire to keep their historic advantages. Minorities may sense this and harbor resentment when change does not occur fast enough.

It is important that these issues be discussed even though it is often difficult to deal with them. Because good race relations are dependent on the goodwill of all the races involved, one may be pessimistic about the development of racial harmony. The more one thinks about ending traditional discrimination so as to bring about equality to all races the more one realizes that all parties must begin to die to their own interests for this goal to succeed.

As Christians we can see that racism and discrimination are not just secular issues but have important spiritual dimensions that must be addressed. The renegotiation of the racial relationship is not going to be done through the law or the state. It is going to encompass a deliberate decision for all of us to work out the problems that have historically crippled our relationships with each other. When we begin to assert the equality of the races, not just in our minds but in our hearts as well, we will finally begin to extinguish the societal expectation of inequality that weighs so heavily on us all. When that occurs, racial reconciliation will at last have taken place. Racial reconciliation, then, is the process by which we overcome the previous dysfunctional, unequal relationship between the races and develop an egalitarian, healthy relationship.

I am convinced that the best place for this renegotiation to begin is in the church. If God's people cannot learn how to get along then what is the hope for anyone? This is going to be a painful process. Truths will have to be spoken, myths will have to be crushed, and feelings will be hurt. Renegotiation is rarely an easy process, especially when it involves races that have been at odds for hundreds of years.

10

Public Problems, Private Solutions

> Today "liberals" are inclined to stress justice more than freedom.
> Conservatives often value freedom more than justice. One crucial test
> of whether Christian political activity is free of ideological bias . . .
> [is] whether it emphasizes both freedom and justice in equal measure.
>
> Ronald Sider
> *Completely Pro-Life*

I sometimes drive my students crazy. Because of my teaching style they often do not know what I really believe. I often take both sides of an issue so that they can get the chance to figure out where they stand without pressure from me.

This technique tends to make students curious about what I truly believe about issues. What political position do I really take? Am I a dittohead? Or am I one of those bleeding heart liberals? I hope no one who is reading this will be in my class anytime soon because I'm going to give the answer I usually keep from students. The answer is yes. I consider myself a political moderate. Sometimes I take the conservative side of an issue and sometimes I take a quite liberal view. To me a real moderate does not just live in the middle but rather retains the flexibility to jump to the left or to the right however his conscience may lead him.

The Christian Conservative

This can make life interesting since most of my Christian friends are quite politically conservative while most of my fellow sociologists are very liberal. I get to see and hear from the best (and sometimes the worst) of both worlds. Maybe that is why I am a moderate. I find that, contrary to what many Christians may believe, my moderate position does not contradict the teachings of the Bible—I totally accept the Bible as the Word of God. Yet I feel free to disagree with conservative Christian friends on many political issues. It seems that we Christians often read our own societal values into the Bible rather than allowing the Bible to determine our values. We turn our perception of God into a reflection of our own personal beliefs.

It is not unlike some liberal churches that refuse to condemn the practice of homosexuality. When we get beyond all of their logical and theological protests, we find that they advocate the gay political agenda because many of their members are homosexuals who do not want to repent of this sin. Therefore, the cultural beliefs of the church members determine their perception of scriptural truth.

However, many conservative Christians act as if God is a strong Republican because they do not want to face the possibility that many of their political positions may be more self-serving than attempts to honor God and serve humanity. Conservatism can become an idol when Christians accept it without question. They begin to worship their conservative projection of our Lord rather than our Lord himself. We need to be careful to acknowledge the difference between our political positions and the teachings found in the Bible. We can "speak for God" only on matters clearly found in his Word.

Perhaps the tendency of many Christians to project their conservative convictions on their theology concerns me because of its implications regarding racial issues. Before I explain that statement I must make a disclaimer. There is no empirical evidence that individuals who are politically conservative are any more racist than those who are politically liberal. Having stated that, I feel that it is necessary to suggest that the politically conservative position that so many Christians cling to has serious flaws when it comes to dealing with racism. A major theme of conservatism is the attempt to find private solutions to society's problems, rather than public ones. Thus there is the promotion of freedom from governmental interference. In many areas of life this is acceptable. It's evident that government legislation will not end racism. Much of racism must be addressed by individuals. However, the extent to which racism has crippled our society makes me think that we should not be too quick to throw away all public solutions.

Affirmative action may be a policy that we have to rethink, but something like it is needed to redress some of the injustices and to level the playing field for all races. If affirmative action is wrong, then we need to think of a better way to accomplish our goals. It is not conservative criticism of affirmative action programs that is a problem; it's the fact that nothing is offered to take their place. It seems that conservatives believe that hundreds of years of oppression can be reversed overnight. A few years of trying a program is long enough, they reason. By then it's obvious that it won't work, or it's working too well and is putting the majority at a disadvantage.

Justice demands that we find a way to create real opportunities for minorities who are suffering from societal disadvantage created by generations of abuse. If justice is to be served, however, we can't create a mechanism that lashes out unfairly against whites. It may be that such a solution cannot be found this side of heaven, but it is our duty to try.

Conservatives who refuse to attempt public remedies and only concentrate on possible private answers are probably not going to find solutions. Because racism is a public problem, there will have to be public aspects to any private solutions we attempt. As Christians we must not become so wedded to conservative political philosophy that we are unable to envision solutions that our Lord may be patiently attempting to convey to us.

So that I will not be misunderstood, let me state that clearly there are problems the state cannot handle. The state can protect me from overt discrimination from the neighbor down the street who hates my guts because I am black but it can never take away that neighbor's hatred. A private solution is needed for that. Individuals within that person's sphere of influence could confront him about his hate.

If we say we believe in private solutions, we must take steps to implement them. If we don't do anything privately, our advocacy of private solutions is merely a covering for our unwillingness to honestly deal with the fact that racism is still a significant problem in society.

I fear that many politically conservative Christians, while not overtly racist, still do not want to admit that racism is a significant problem in this nation because that admission might threaten their political belief system. For example, many believe that if we left things up to market forces somehow justice would prevail. It's been shown, however, that market forces inevitably aid those who are already in advantageous places in society. Thus the marketplace will usually favor whites over minorities because of the historic discrimination minorities have faced. If conservatives admit that racial minorities still do not have the same opportunities to succeed as whites, they have to admit that the marketplace by itself cannot solve racism. As Christians we must be honest. We must acknowledge racism when it exists and do something about it, bringing about repentance and reconciliation.

There is nothing wrong with a Christian holding on to conservative political values. I share many of those values. But the Christian must be flexible enough in his or her thinking to let go of those values when they get in the way of godly solutions. Before Christians will be ready to honestly deal with racism in society, they have to open themselves to the possibility that some of their beliefs concerning race and politics may be faulty or incomplete. It is only when we recognize that we may be going down the wrong path that we are able to assess the path and adjust our direction.

11

The Music of the Streets

Souljah was not born to make white people feel comfortable. . . .
And if my survival means your destruction, then so be it.
                                                        Sister Souljah

Gangsta rap! It is rapidly replacing rock as the music that is most
dreaded by Christian youth ministers. The controversy surrounding the
album "Cop Killer" is similar to the hostility from some quarters toward the
rock group KISS in the early part of their career. Older adults are often not
sure what is actually being said in the songs and they do not trust the artists.
Adults were concerned about messages of sexuality and the occult in rock
songs and now fear the messages of violence and hatred in gangsta rap. Conservative commentators such as Rush Limbaugh are quick to use this type
of music as examples of black racism toward whites. Despite all the turmoil
that has developed around it, this music has grown in popularity. In fact I
suspect that the controversy may have encouraged the popularity.

To understand the celebrity of this music we must try to put ourselves
into the mindset of those who are the major consumers of it. Many of
these would be lower class, urban African Americans. Such music touches
on an ideology that gives them hope by explaining their difficult situation in ways that make sense to them. According to rap lyrics, the reason why racial minorities are suffering is due to the racist structures that
have been put in place by whites. Whites can no longer make blacks into
slaves or overtly oppress them through Jim Crow laws, but they can keep
blacks in their place with brutal policemen and a crooked legal system.
If nothing else, the tape of the Rodney King beating confirms the belief
of blacks that they are more likely to suffer abuse than whites would in
similar situations. Empirical sociological evidence also confirms that our
system of justice is skewed against blacks.

Gangsta rap offers a way out for the urban black. It expresses many of the sentiments these individuals feel. The lyrics generally adhere to a black nationalist ideology and thus talk about race relations as if the races were two armies at war with each other. Indeed this ideology assumes that we are in a subtle (and sometimes not so subtle) race war where whites have taken the initiative through racist institutions. The solution then is for blacks and other racial minorities to take up arms and physically fight this race war. Riots are not an unfortunate phenomenon but the natural development of war. The killing of a cop is not necessarily wrong because it can be seen as an act of self-defense or a normal casualty of war.

Is this chilling prescription the rantings of a few extremists? Unfortunately this philosophy is not as rare as one might hope. The popularity of black leaders such as Louis Farrakhan reveals the inroads this ideology has made in the black community. Furthermore, unlike many of the white supremacist groups, many of the leaders of these groups are well educated. Since intellectuals are defenders of this ideology, it will not be easily dislodged from the black community. In some ways in our current society, it may be easier for blacks to adhere to an overt racist ideology than for whites.

Is such an ideology fair? Is it right? Of course it is not. This may not be a healthy ideology but it apparently meets certain desires of some African Americans as evidenced by the proliferation of racial rap in the black community.

A couple of these desires have already been suggested. For example, this ideology allows blacks to feel empowered to fight against whites. To a lower class black who sees very few legitimate chances for advancement, the ability to fight the ones who are perceived to have placed him or her in the position of depravity can encourage that person and even give him hope. Therefore the black nationalist ideology can give blacks a goal, a way to focus their anger.

This ideology also allows blacks to explain the societal and personal problems in their lives without their having to take a major amount of responsibility for those problems. Why are so many blacks in jail? Why are there so many unemployed? Why is the black family falling apart? It is the fault of whites who happen to have the lion's share of the power in our culture. To take power away from such evil forces works to the greater good of blacks, and the overthrow of white power by whatever means necessary is legitimated. This neatly allows the African American to justify any current personal shortcomings in his or her life and to justify future actions that work to pull whites out of the structures of power.

59

It should not be a surprise that an ideology of black racism has developed. For the past four hundred years, whites have been demonstrating for blacks systems of racism. My own ancestors were shipped like cattle to this country, owned like property, eventually given second-class citizenship, and still today I am barred from complete acceptance into modern society. I often find myself having to disprove the black stereotypes of laziness or ignorance. Almost daily I have to deal with the obvious fear that some white strangers display in my presence, just because I'm a black man. Gangsta rap and organizations such as the Nation of Islam have become important outlets for many blacks, helping them deal with the injustices they experience every day.

What has the moral agent of society, the Christian church, done about all of these atrocities? The Christian church played a part in establishing the abolition movement and to a lesser degree participated in the early Civil Rights movement. However, it is fair to say that the church has not done nearly enough of what it should do to bring about racial justice. Even today the leaders of the church remain silent on the subject of racism. For fear of being stung, they prefer not to disturb the nest of racial bias that lies within the hearts of many pew sitters.

Christians should not be surprised to see many young blacks running away from the church for solace. When the church does not strive to bring justice to individuals who have been disadvantaged, those individuals will find other sources of help. If we care about ministering to people of different races, we must begin to find ways in the church to address issues of stratification and discrimination.

The church can no longer be silent regarding racism. If we wait to speak up, extremist groups will have gained a powerful foothold. We must attempt to find ways to intentionally counter racism now. It is no surprise that an inner-city black youth listens to a black man who is singing or talking about the very problems that face blacks every day. It's no surprise that an inner-city black youth turns off the white man who only criticizes the songs and ideology that champion blacks. The mission of white Christians is to demonstrate the love and compassion of our Lord. In time I believe our Lord can use that love to turn the hearts of blacks, twisted by hatred, away from the forces that feed that hatred. That may only come when the Christian church begins to adopt an attitude of true repentance and reconciliation. We cannot manufacture this attitude on our own but, praise God, it is a gift that our heavenly Father gives to those who are ready to receive it.

PART 2

MORE
than
REGRET

If a man becomes interested in a woman, it is wise for him to find out about that woman's past relationships. If she has been mistreated by other men, she may bring the repercussions of those interactions into the new relationship. She can easily associate anything her new boyfriend does with the negative qualities of her former boyfriends. Women are not the only ones who do this. I have found myself being wary of both romantic and nonromantic situations that are similar to circumstances where I experienced pain. We all bring the baggage of past relationships into present situations.

The racial question is about relationships. Relationships between the races are not what the Lord intended them to be. We can hope that the future will bring improvement but we cannot forget the past. The past has given us what we now endure and what we will have to deal with in the future. Therefore we must do more than merely regret what has happened in the past.

We must honestly confront the past so that we can work with the Lord to create a new future.

It's always easier to just ignore the past. We just state how awful things used to be and thank God they are not that bad today. If our Lord had taken such a tactic with us, would we have the chance for reconciliation to him? Would we have the opportunity to escape our sin nature? When we merely ignore past sins in the hope that their effects will go away, we are creating situations that guarantee the return of those sins.

If we are going to deal with racism in our society, we are going to have to take an activist approach. It is only when we come to terms with the sins of the past that we can eradicate the effects of those transgressions in the present. Regret of sin is necessary but it is only the first step.

12

I Don't Need
Racial Reconciliation

> This is white man's Christian religion used to brainwash us black people. . . . this blue-eyed devil has twisted his Christianity to keep his foot on our backs . . . to keep our eyes fixed on the pie in the sky, and heaven in the hereafter, . . . while right here . . . on this earth . . . in this life.
>
> Malcolm X
> *The Autobiography of Malcolm X*

I am having a hard time sleeping tonight. I had a disturbing conversation with a black man not too long ago. It makes me pessimistic that we can ever have racial harmony. This is what he said:

"Racial reconciliation? Racial reconciliation! Don't give me any grief about working for racial reconciliation. What do I need racial reconciliation for? I am a black male who is just trying to survive in this white society. That is all the racial reconciliation I need. Don't tell me to work for something I receive every day whether I want it or not.

"You see, I am already as reconciled to whites as I ever want to be. I am not free to live out the culture that I grew up with. I have to come into white society and adjust to what whites want. Any African American who has experienced any sort of success knows what I'm talking about. If you want to make it in America, you have to go to a white college and learn how to act 'white.' If you don't, nobody will hire you no matter how qualified you are. They will label you as 'rebellious.' You must dress like a white man, talk like one, joke like one, and even think like one to a certain degree. I can tell you all about the white culture because I am forced to imitate that culture to get at the resources that whites control.

63

But because we blacks don't control many resources, most whites could not tell you anything about *my* culture except what they have seen in the movies. I have enough racial reconciliation. I don't need any more.

"Any black who is honest will tell you that reconciliation is just another trap that whites can use to get what they want from blacks. You don't believe me? Just look at what has happened to our black women. During slavery they were just playthings for the white man. He could do anything he wanted with them as long as he did not give them the honor of marrying them. Even after blacks were freed, it was not uncommon to see white men use power, money, and intimidation to gain access to black women. But if any black man even looked at a white woman, he could expect to find a rope around his neck. The white man was not interested in loving the black woman. He probably thought he was doing her a favor by sleeping with her. He was not interested in an equal relationship. This was his idea of reconciliation. Why should I believe that he is interested in an equal relationship today? On what basis do I believe that whites are not merely seeking another way to gain what they want from blacks through this racial reconciliation? They just want us to lower our guard so they can take the little we have left. I don't need any of this racial reconciliation.

"Some say we need to be grateful to whites who want racial reconciliation, that if whites are willing to forsake some of their prestige to come and be with us, then we should be happy. We should be grateful for any of the material resources that whites offer us. Why? The way I figure it, anything whites give they owed us. My ancestors did not ask to be stacked like logs in a ship and dragged over here, naked and malnourished, to work on the plantations of white men. We did not ask for a life of oppression and abuse for the sake of building the infrastructure of this country. We did not want to neglect the education and development of our children, but we have been denied the opportunity to protect our families and have been pushed to the bottom rung of society. The way I figure it, anything we gain from whites is something they owe us for centuries of our giving our lives to build this country without just compensation. If you are really interested in justice, don't worry about this fancy concept of racial reconciliation and just give me what you owe me. I don't need any of this racial reconciliation.

"Why does the victim need to be reconciled to the villain? The villain is just trying to convince the victim that reconciliation is needed so he can get off easy. If the villain can convince the victim that reconciliation is necessary, he can get that victim to say 'I forgive you' without demanding anything other than a shallow apology. In this way the conscience of the villain is appeased, but the victim has gained almost nothing in the exchange. It's a rip-off. I am a black man. I am a victim. I do not gain anything from reconciliation. This is just a ploy to appease the consciences of those who have historically abused me and continue to hold me 'in my place.' I don't need any of this racial reconciliation.

"Don't get me wrong. I am not saying that I am perfect or anything. There are times when I need reconciliation, times when I've done something wrong. In racial matters I am innocent so reconciliation is not needed, but when I have done wrong to someone else, I will seek reconciliation. I am not a monster who rejects the need in relationships for apologies and forgiveness. I merely reserve those efforts for times when it is right. When I am in the wrong, I will seek to make things right.

"For example, I once had an accident with my mom's car. No one was seriously hurt but the car was nearly totaled. At first I thought it was the other guy's fault. But later I realized that I was at fault. It cost my mother a lot of money to fix the other man's car. It was a lot of money she didn't have. She managed to scrape it up, but I know that it really hurt her financially for a while. Now that was a time where I needed reconciliation. I was at fault and I took full responsibility for the mess that I put my mother in. By taking full responsibility for my actions, I assured that my relationship with my mother could stay close.

"I know what you're thinking. You're thinking that I was not the only one who helped to maintain that relationship. My mom had to forgive me and not hold a grudge or this accident could have been held over my head and we would not have been reconciled. Well of course that's true. But she is my mother and that is what she's supposed to do. She loves me and love is the force behind forgiveness anyway. It is not like she owed it to me but she is my mother and a mother doesn't want to lose a relationship with her son. So in that sense she gained something by forgiving me, even though I didn't earn her forgiveness. She gained the continued relationship with her son.

"What can I gain from forgiving whites? If my mother had not forgiven me, we might have eventually blown this issue up to the point where we no longer had a relationship with each other. The past would continue to contaminate our future together. We would be hurting each other with denunciations about each other to other members of the family. We probably would make the rest of our family miserable. I guess we both had a lot to gain through the process of reconciliation. Funny, on the surface one would naturally think that I was the main beneficiary of this reconciliation process. But in truth, it is not only me and my mother, but our whole family who gained quite a bit through our reconciliation.

"Is it possible that blacks can gain something through racial reconciliation? Is there something more to be gained for us out of racial relations than material redistribution? Material redistribution and more societal power are what the majority of our black leaders are fighting for. But are they enough? Can we gain something from the restoration of the relationship that whites and blacks have allowed to be torn apart? Indeed, will all the individuals in society gain from black-white reconciliation? In light of these thoughts racial reconciliation may take on a heightened sense of importance.

"Maybe there is more to be gained in racial reconciliation than the pacifying of white guilt. It may be that the very concept of restoring a relationship can offer African Americans something that we have not had before. Maybe we African Americans can gain rest from our anger. Hatred, even if justified, can be a tiring emotion and a heavy burden to carry around. The opportunity to set down this burden and be free to love whomever I want to love regardless of past abuses is an awfully tempting offer at times.

"But how can I free myself from this hatred? When I look at my own experiences and my knowledge of black history, I know that whites are not to be trusted. Whenever they offer me a worm, I must look for the hook. If only I could really believe that whites are sincere when they talk about racial reconciliation. If only I could believe that they are not merely trying to be 'politically correct' and gain some sort of emotional rush from being forgiven by blacks. If only I could believe that affirmative action programs are more than ways to satisfy white guilt for how their past abuses have created the black underclass. Then it might be possible to believe that whites who talk of brotherhood are not merely attempting to stop me from seeking retribution. Then I could finally put down the defenses that I have erected against whites and accept them as true companions. It is only at that point that I will be truly free from the horror of America's racial past.

"Racial reconciliation? Freedom? Can it be that these two concepts go together for blacks? I can choose to hold on to bitterness or I can risk gaining freedom from my hatred. But is it worth the risk? If white Americans are not really interested in racial reconciliation then I'd better keep up my defenses. That is the only way I can assure myself of not being burned. But if they really are willing to be honest about our racial past, then I too may gain more than an 'I'm sorry.' I can finally put an end to my anger and can learn how to truly love all people. They will benefit as well. They will gain more than superficial forgiveness; they have the possibility of gaining real friends. True reconciliation is always beneficial to all parties involved.

"That then is my dilemma. Only the white person can allow me to be rid of my hatred, because it is only when whites are honest about their guilt that I am going to be honest about my bitterness. And it is only when there is that sort of honesty that the possibility of relationship becomes real. Do I take this risk? Will the white person truly seek reconciliation this time or will he once again seek to use the situation to his advantage? Unlike past encounters concerning race, this time we may both clearly see that we need each other. As a black man, I have a role to play in reconciliation. If I do not play that role, reconciliation becomes impossible. Then the races are condemned to continue the cycles of hatred and mistrust that we have established so well. We may survive, but only in terror of each other. And the whole family of races will suffer in the balance.

"Maybe there is something to this racial reconciliation, because for once both races would be forced to work together to achieve a goal that would benefit each other. It is something that whites cannot do alone. It is something that they must do by interacting and cooperating with us to create a new relationship. By giving ourselves to each other we may finally be free from the burden of our collective past and be able to forge a new future.

"Yet how can I ever trust whites and allow such reconciliation to take place? Even if I want reconciliation, I have my doubts that it will ever be possible. And if it is not possible, why try to get along with white people?"

13

Can I Understand the Klan?

> For though I am free from all men, I have made myself a slave to all,
> that I might win the more. And to the Jews I became as a Jew, that
> I might win Jews; to those who are under the Law, as under the Law,
> . . . that I might win those who are under the Law. . . . I have become
> all things to all men, that I may by all means save some.
>
> 1 Corinthians 9:19–20, 22

It is so hard to understand the feelings and ideas of individuals who come from backgrounds that are very different from ours. A black radical, such as the one in the last chapter, brings to us a reality that is unfamiliar to most whites. Many would ask, "How can we have reconciliation if there are minorities like that one?" A good question. To reverse this question I can ask, "How can racial harmony be possible in light of the continued existence of the Ku Klux Klan?" Obviously racial reconciliation is going to be difficult to accomplish.

Sociologists talk about "taking the mind of the other." This is the process of trying to interpret from his or her point of view the actions and attitudes of another person. This process is invaluable in helping us understand other cultures. As Christians we are to love and try to identify with others. This technique can help us do that. It can give us insight into the thinking of our brothers and sisters of different races. Our understanding the Klansman and the black radical may not bring them to a position of racial tolerance, but it allows for the possibility of working with them toward this goal instead of always fighting against them.

Is it possible for a black man to become sympathetic to a member of the Klan? I do not know if I could ever sympathize with such individuals. It's easier for me to relate to the black radical, although I disagree with most of what he says. But it is possible for me to understand why individuals might join the Klan. In fact I believe that I have gained some insight into this.

Austin, Texas, must be the most politically liberal city in Texas, so you can imagine my surprise when I found out that the Klan was going to hold a rally at the state capitol building. At first I reacted to the idea with disgust. But then I decided that I ought to go to the rally. After all, I had never seen a Klan rally before and I am almost always ready for a new experience! In a weird way, it could actually be fun. (I know. My elevator does not always go all the way to the top!)

On the day of the rally the site became a party spot for progressive and liberal activists. Political groups from gay rights to radical black organizations gathered with the purpose of shouting down the Klan speakers. The city had wisely taken the precaution of surrounding the rally area with the biggest police officers they could find, all dressed in riot gear. I knew that the rally was about to start when those officers snapped to attention.

The speaker for the Klan was obviously an ignorant man. I do not say that in a derogatory manner but I could tell from his speech that he did not have much education, not that it really mattered. It was hard to hear him because all the activists were making as much noise as they could. Several were beating drums in an attempt to disrupt the proceedings.

I could only hear about half of what the Klansman was saying. It was the usual rhetoric, but then the guy made a statement that made me think. He spoke directly to his potential followers. I looked out among the crowd and put myself in "the mind of the other." The other was a white man in the crowd who appeared to be down on his luck. I guessed that he was not well educated. Perhaps his wife had just left him or he had just lost his job. He was probably responsible for his lot in life; however, like the rest of us, he did not easily take responsibility for his actions. He never felt like he had much power in his life.

It was easy for him to believe the general racial stereotypes about minorities that he heard in the media and from his peers. He'd never had any good minority friends. The vast majority of the racial minorities that he knew, he knew only briefly.

Perhaps such a man has always distrusted minorities but has never been in a position to do much with that distrust beyond a personal level. He has come to this rally with preconceived ideas that racial minorities have brought about much of his unpleasant situation. Maybe a black man got his job. Or there is strife with his wife over the Hispanics who just moved

69

to his neighborhood. He did not come to this rally ready to totally accept all that the Klansmen had to say but he is looking for answers.

He's bothered by the black radicals who are making so much noise. He cannot hear the speaker who has the answers he needs. This is not right in his eyes. And it is just more proof that racial minorities have taken control of our society while sticking it to poor slobs like him. How has being white helped him?

At this point the man may begin to sympathize with the Klan. After all, they are like him. Their enemies appear to be the same ones who have tormented him. He is now open to believing whatever they have to say. In time he may contact them and hear their explanations for the problems of society, namely that lower class whites are being victimized by powerful minority-oriented social movements. He is also open to the solution that they propose—that whites must regain power in their country if they are to survive. As he becomes more active within this group he will develop what we call "cognitive dissonance." This is the tendency to shape our beliefs to be in harmony with our actions. Thus to justify joining a supremacist group he actually begins to believe that whites are the superior race and that minorities are ruining this country.

I do not empathize with this man. There is no emotional connection from me to him. Yet, in a strange way, I understand why he feels the way he does. In a situation where he feels that he has no power, the Klan seems to offer him a way to gain power. He has found a way to thumb his nose at a system that seems to have mistreated him. I do not condone the racist actions that he undertakes but I realize that those actions are connected to many of the same fears that we all share.

Can understanding this man help me show him the error of his ways? Not likely. Just as some tragedy in his life likely opened him up to accepting racist ideology, it will take another major personal event for him to rethink that ideology. Bringing about such events is the responsibility of the Lord, not me. Hopefully at such a time there will be a caring Christian, probably white, who can help him work himself out of the racist trap that he finds himself in. We should never discount the power of our Lord to work incredible miracles in people's hearts, helping them deal with their racism. More than once, I have heard of a black leading a white racist to Christ or a white leading a black radical to faith in our Lord.

What good is it for me to try to understand a racist? If I can understand why a person is racist then I may be less likely to continue the cycle of hatred that would go on between us. It is harder to hate that which you understand. As a Christian, I am called to love, not hate. Christ's call to love is not limited to those with whom I agree or who are easy to love. It is also not a call to merely tolerate them. I must learn to love the man who joins the Klan. Understanding him is an important first step if I am to reach a point where I really care about him.

If I hate this man it will have a negative effect on my relationships with other whites. I may be suspicious of them and they of me. This is no way to bring about reconciliation.

By trying to understand this man, I will begin to understand the fears that drive him and many whites in their interactions with minorities. Down the line, when I encounter these fears, I will not be taken by surprise. Hopefully I will be able to respond with sensitivity and compassion, and my reaction may help someone overcome his or her racism. They, in turn, may help me to deal with my fears.

Finally, it is important to note that as long as we are unwilling to try to understand why others may feel the way they do, we will tend to stereotype others in ways that are not fair. It is so easy for me to just write off our friend in the Klan as a hateful, ignorant bigot and believe that all he wants is a return to the days of Jim Crow laws so that he can feel superior to me. Undoubtedly there are individuals in the Klan who feel that way. Yet I suspect that many are haunted by the fears I have touched on and have just needed a scapegoat. And, as we know, minorities make good scapegoats. As a Christian, I must try to see our Klansman as a human being, not a stereotype, or I may fall into the sin of creating a scapegoat. It's easy to hate a stereotype. But with a human being it's possible to have understanding, reconciliation, and even fellowship.

14

Finger Pointing

> You hypocrite, first take the log out of your own eye, and then you
> will see clearly to take the speck out of your brother's eye.
>
> Matthew 7:5

Maybe it is because I am an African American, but I find it particularly distressing when minority students do worse in my class than the white students. I never enjoy failing a student, but the use of the failing grade is necessary for students who cannot or will not do the work required to show mastery of a subject. I still find it particularly difficult to use this tool on minority students.

Do not misunderstand me. I do not give any of my minority students any breaks. A student's grade is determined only by my assessment of the scholarly work that the student has done. I will not cheapen one individual's grade by giving it to other individuals who have not earned it. Besides, I do not feel that I am really doing a student a favor if I pass him or her when the student hasn't done what is required to pass. Someone else will probably have to flunk that student later.

Lower Test Scores

Studies have shown that minority students (except for Asians) do not do as well in school as white students. Minorities are more likely to drop out of school and they get lower grades. My experience as a professor has confirmed this finding. I wonder why this is so. Are minority students really inferior to whites?

Perhaps the reason why minority students do not perform well can partly be found in the differential in SAT scores that we see between minority and white students. The average score of Asians is the highest, followed by whites, Hispanics, and blacks. Despite the differences in test scores many minority students enter college, and this accounts for much of the differential in performance that students of different races exhibit at the college level. What do these SAT score differentials mean? Do some races have more mental ability than others? I can never prove that biology does not somehow play a role but I do not think that this is the major catalyst of this phenomenon.

The different experiences that each group has undergone in our society may contribute to the apparent differences. There is little doubt that part of the explanation for this discrepancy is generated by the oppression and discrimination that minorities have suffered. Historical disadvantage cannot be erased overnight—or even over a generation. Members of different ethnic groups do not have the same starting point in our race to achieve educational success. Those who believe that we do are deceiving themselves. To the degree that SAT scores reveal the effects of lingering prejudice and discrimination in our society, we should expect that such scores will favor whites over minorities. Thus SAT scores may reflect the broader racial reality that exists in our society today.

As Christians it is our responsibility to correct such historical wrongs. We must acknowledge the evil that our past has created—not so we can pile on guilt, but so we can find creative solutions to these problems. Such solutions may be costly. Repentance and recommitment to what is right often are costly. Maybe superficial programs like affirmative action must be replaced with long-term investment in developing the resources of our minority citizens. We may have to question the role white flight has played in contributing to this problem and how our private Christian schools often exacerbate the situation. We cannot ignore the racism that pervades our society and how it has altered the fortunes of many minorities.

There are serious problems with this oppression thesis, however. First, it does not explain why Asian Americans do so well academically. While the types of oppression that each race has historically faced differ, no one can deny that Asian Americans have faced severe discrimination in our nation. Furthermore, many of these Asian students come from the same schools that many of the black students come from yet they consistently outperform white students on all empirical measures.

Second, black and Hispanic students do worse than white students even when we look at students from the same income class. Discrimination has kept minority students from the advantages of monetary privilege such as good schools, but they should perform as well as white students at similar levels of income who also attended inferior schools. Studies do not bear this out.

Unpopular Explanations

I find myself drawn to a conclusion that I am loath to admit. In fact if I were white I would probably be accused of being a racist for drawing this conclusion. As it is, I will probably be accused of being an Uncle Tom black. My conclusion is that not all of the racial differences that I see in my classroom can be accounted for by societal discrimination. I also do not believe that biological abilities explain these differences. I am forced to conclude that part of the explanation lies in the African American and the Mexican American cultures. In some way we are teaching our kids lessons that inhibit their ability to succeed. These lessons probably suppress their ability to succeed not only in college but also in other aspects of life.

I am not ashamed of my black heritage. It is not easy to admit that something that helps to define my African American experience also works to deny many of my brothers and sisters the opportunity to succeed. It is similar to denying a part of myself. But I must be honest if I am going to be able to get at the root of what has gone terribly wrong with many of my African American students. I must be honest enough to follow the evidence that might lead to a solution to this problem. And that evidence seems to indicate that blacks live in a culture that somehow disadvantages them in this society.

What is it in our collective experience as blacks in America that contributes to our academic failings? Part of the answer may lie in the concept of self-efficacy. As we have seen, researchers have found many blacks suffer from a lack of self-efficacy. They have a fatalistic attitude, not believing that their efforts in life will be rewarded.

If we look at the history of African Americans in our nation, it is not hard to see why such a trait may have developed within our culture. One of the characteristics of many slaves is the loss of hope of ever being free. Obviously such an attitude is encouraged by slave owners as fatalistic slaves are less likely to rebel or to try to escape. Even after slavery there was great effort to keep African Americans in their place. One of the primary purposes of lynchings was to show the African American community the result of not keeping in their proper place. With such a historical background there is little doubt as to why low self-efficacy is prevalent within the black population.

This low self-efficacy would account for blacks' not doing well at school. It would reflect an unwillingness of African Americans to give their best effort at universities. If you believe that you are going to fail anyway, why try your best? That way, when you do fail, at least you can say that you did not try your best and avert the appearance of being inferior in ability. We can accuse the system for our failure instead. Group preference can erase individual shortcomings. Being black provides us with a convenient excuse for our failure so that we do not have to acknowledge it.

Our African American culture may contribute to this problem in another way. We cling to our status as victims. Shelby Steele argues that blacks desire to gain power and do so by emphasizing how much they are victims in our society.[1] To the degree that blacks gain power because of the legitimacy of their claims to victimization, they have an incentive to prove how society has deprived them. Poor blacks, then, instead of successful ones, are held up as being typical. African Americans who are able to succeed are ignored as possible role models since they disprove the myth that success in this country is impossible for blacks.

Anyone who has worked with African American youth can readily see the effects of this phenomenon. Students who do well in school are ridiculed. The goal is to get by with as little work as possible. Such an attitude easily leads to substandard academic work and a population ill-prepared for higher education. When these individuals go on to college and flunk out, they often quickly blame the white establishment instead of their own attitudes toward education. Let me make this clear. I have no sympathy for any minority who fails to use his or her abilities to their fullest extent and then wants to blame whites for his or her failure. I will flunk them out of my class just as fast as any white professor would. If we are going to find reconciliation in this society, we African Americans are going to have to take responsibility for our own actions.

Perhaps there are important lessons to be learned from my experience with my minority students. Perhaps the most important is that rarely can any one phenomenon be explained by one factor. White racism, by itself, cannot explain the failure of minority students. The culture of the minorities must take some of the blame. Therefore we must look at how we can encourage our children at a young age to attain academic success. The norms and values that sustain our inability to compete with the dominant white culture must be replaced with those that will enable us to excel in that culture. We will not totally deny our African American culture but we must be honest and flexible enough to modify elements within it that work to our disadvantage. It can be done. The experience of Asian Americans proves this.

I have thought about why I was not trapped into a fatalistic attitude toward education. Why do I not have low self-efficacy? An important part of the answer is my mother. She encouraged me to excel at school at a very early age. She encouraged me to read and go to the library. I felt very competent in school and was encouraged to do my best. She eventually went back to school and received her teaching degree. As a teacher she has confirmed to me that it is the students whose parents become involved with their schooling that succeed in her class. That certainly is one of the keys.

Parental involvement in education is not an exclusive value for whites or Asians. It must become a value within our African American culture if we are going to make the changes that we have to make to correct the racial inequality we experience here in America. Yes, we blacks have a responsibility in bringing racial equality to our society. We cannot just badger whites into doing it. We must work at helping ourselves. When you think about it, it is only when we prepare ourselves to the same extent that white students do that equality of opportunity will have any sort of meaning.

We must all work together to eradicate all of the old systems of racism and hatred that linger in our society. We must also be honest in assessing the damage that many minorities do to themselves. Finger pointing is meaningless for minorities if we are not willing to work hard ourselves. If we do not take advantage of our present opportunities why should society give us further opportunities? We will only be equals when we have worked to make ourselves equal. Laws can give us opportunities but not the resolve to use those opportunities. It is only as equals that we can eventually develop the sorts of solutions that can bring reconciliation and justice to our society.

15

A Book by Its Cover

> Therefore do not go on passing judgment before the time, but wait until the Lord comes who will both bring to light the things hidden in the darkness and disclose the motives of men's hearts; and then each man's praise will come to him from God.
>
> 1 Corinthians 4:5

I spent one year of my life working as a substitute teacher. I know bad people will go to hell. I'm convinced that *really bad* people will become substitute teachers! To be honest, probably at least part of the misery that I experienced that year was payback for the horrid way I treated my substitute teachers when I was in school. This confirms yet another truth in the Bible: You sow the wind and you will reap the whirlwind (see Hosea 8:7). Or what goes around comes around.

When I went into a new class as a substitute teacher, the first question my students usually asked me was not my name. The first question usually was: "Do you play basketball?" Now in the right context this is a valid question. It can even be a compliment. If I am walking down the street in shorts and a T-shirt, then the question implies that people see that my body is in good shape. I am somewhat athletic and I would enjoy that compliment. However, when I am in a suit and about to teach, this question has another meaning. It reflects the common image of African Americans that our society has developed. I ask myself: Would they have asked that question if I were white? While tall—six feet, three inches—I'm not unusually tall. So where does this question come from?

In the movie *Soul Man* everyone wants a man, who they think is black, to play on their basketball team. The problem is the man is white. He just took an overdose of tanning pills and resembles a black man. He turned out to be a terrible basketball player. The comedy is that the assumptions we make about others often prove to be untrue.

So why does it bother me if individuals believe me to be a good basketball player? What I'm reacting to is the stereotype of black men: They are quite gifted athletically but not too smart. They have great sexual prowess but they are also quite lazy. And they tend to be criminally minded. My fear is that individuals who accept one dimension of this stereotype will accept other dimensions of it that are not as flattering. For example, sometimes on the street, a white man will say to me something like, "What's happening?" or "What's up?" in an attempt at street vernacular. He assumes that I have a certain attitude and manner without even knowing me. He speaks to me as though I am "cool" and also probably lazy and uneducated. His assumptions are false. My speech has developed through more than twenty years of schooling, not from the latest slang on the streets.

As much as I enjoy basketball and many other sports, I feel that my personality is molded more by my academic and spiritual pursuits than by my athletic ones. Yet those who choose to stereotype me will miss those sides of me and choose to focus on my athletic side because this is what they expect from me. That is one of the major problems with stereotyping. It fails to take the entire person into account. It seems so easy to reduce a person to a stereotype. That way we can feel that we understand who that person is and do not have to bother to allow that person to show us who he or she fully is. An important step to learning to appreciate our brothers and sisters from different races is for all of us to take the time to find out who they really are.

Once we have placed individuals into a given stereotype, we then become very adept at finding evidence that confirms our stereotype. For example, if we believe that all Hispanics are uneducated, we will have a tendency to pay attention to situations when the education of an Hispanic individual seems inadequate. And we tend to forget situations when the opposite is true, when the Hispanic individual seems to be very well educated. The human animal has an amazing capacity to generate assumptions and to bias the evidence so as to prove those assumptions true. If we see any evidence that might imply the inferior education of Hispanics, we're quick to plaster labels of ignorance on all Hispanics whether they deserve it or not. We cheat them of the opportunity to reveal their true selves and we cheat ourselves out of the opportunity to make accurate assessments.

The media portray an unflattering image of African Americans and other minorities.[1] The African American male stereotype is one that emphasizes an animalistic nature. One can easily make the case that the police officers who dealt with Rodney King and the jury that freed them reacted more to the fear produced by that image of the African American male than to the facts of the case. One of the reasons that African Americans have never had true equality in America is because we are so often treated as a stereotype rather than as multi-dimensional people.

African Americans have struggled to eradicate this stereotype from the culture, not only to improve their image among whites but also to preserve their own self-esteem. In 1941 James Bayton's classic study showed that more than 60 percent of the black college students he examined accepted an inferior image of blacks as well as a superior image of whites.[2] Another study showed that black children identified with a black doll but, when given a choice, they preferred a white doll over the black one.[3] These studies are old but some of the results have been replicated in a more recent study of preschool children.[4]

There is a disturbing lack of concern on the part of evangelical churches about the problem of stereotyping. Can you remember a sermon or Bible study that pointed out the many ways stereotyping can inhibit our relationships? Was racial stereotyping ever mentioned in that lesson? If the white church wants to attract African Americans as members, it must make a concerted effort to stop stereotyping and to speak out against stereotyping. Members in the church must take the time to discover each person as a unique individual, regardless of skin color.

16

Black Quarterbacks

> The eye cannot say to the hand, "I don't need you!" And the head cannot say to the feet, "I don't need you!" On the contrary, those parts of the body that seem to be weaker are indispensable.
>
> 1 Corinthians 12:21–22 NIV

If you are any kind of a football fan, you know about Warren Moon. He is the former Houston Oiler quarterback. Now he plays for the Minnesota Vikings. I am a fan of his, not only because he is a great quarterback and a fierce competitor, but also because he gives a lot back to the community. Living in Houston for five months I became an Oiler fan in the mid-'80s and have followed Moon ever since then. I think his abilities have been underrated. There are two reasons for this: first, because the Oilers always seem to find a way to lose playoff games (don't remind me of the 1993 Buffalo game when we blew a thirty-two-point lead!); second, because he spent the first five years of his career playing football in Canada. His team even won the Canadian version of the Super Bowl at least once while he was there. Consequently his stats in the NFL, while impressive, do not reflect all of his accomplishments in professional football. I heard an announcer once say that if Moon had played his first five years in the NFL instead of in the Canadian Football League, he would have passed for more yards than any other quarterback in the history of football.

The story of why Moon went to Canada is an interesting one. He was a great quarterback in college, but when he became available for the NFL, blacks were not often used as quarterbacks. The NFL scouts were looking to make him a defensive back or a wide receiver, but Moon does not have blazing speed. He has an accurate, strong arm and a sharp mind. These are the qualities that you want in a quarterback. Moon skipped out on the NFL and played football as a quarterback in Canada instead. He was the best quarterback in that league for five years. When his contract expired, the NFL was more willing to play a black at quarterback and Moon's credentials were good so he came back to the NFL.

Tracking

Moon's story reveals a reality about the NFL in specific and American culture in general. There is often an unspoken yet powerful bias against African Americans when it comes to positions of authority. Sociologists call the phenomenon where individuals from certain races are restricted from certain positions "tracking." For years it was clear that many blacks who were fine college quarterbacks would not get the chance in the NFL. The rationale was always that their athletic ability dictated that they should play a position that was more physically demanding than mentally challenging. Of course such reasoning is faulty. There is not a more important position on the football field than quarterback. If the quarterback is a great athlete as well as an intelligent ballplayer then that is even more of an advantage for the team. But such logic failed to move many African Americans into starting quarterback positions.

Quarterbacks like Moon and Randall Cunningham may have broken the tradition of tracking in the NFL. But we should not totally fault the NFL for allowing such a color line to remain for such a long time. After all, the NFL was merely reflecting the beliefs of the rest of society. Blacks are not generally thought of as leaders, individuals who can think quickly and accurately. Because of this stereotype African Americans often do not gain an opportunity to use their abilities to their full advantage. When this happens, African Americans are not the only ones who are harmed. The very organization that they are attempting to serve is harmed as well.

Let's go back to Moon. The fact that the Houston Oilers did not have Moon playing quarterback the first five years of his career made them a weaker team during that time. Anytime our society takes away the opportunity for individuals to develop to their full potential in the position for which they are naturally suited, our society is weaker for it.

Tracking in the Church

This same type of bias can be seen in our churches. We are robbing ourselves of the best talent we have because we succumb to tracking in

81

church leadership just as in society. In one church an interim youth minister was almost denied the opportunity to become the permanent youth minister because he was black. And this was for a multiracial youth group. I know of another situation where a black man was denied the opportunity to minister in his church because he married a white woman. Each situation is a classic waste of resources. To accomplish all that our Lord has for us to do, the church has no resources to waste.

It's true that you can often survive even when wasting your resources. But usually you don't really enjoy that survival. As a broke college student I often had to undergo periods of poverty in which my main meals consisted of beans and rice. This often happened toward the end of the month. When on the first day of the next month I was paid, I would rush out to buy food. One time, as I was putting away my groceries, I noticed a rather large chunk of ice in the back of the freezer. Curious, I loosened the chunk and pulled it out. Underneath the ice was an unopened package of ham! I had been surviving on beans and rice while a delicious and succulent ham sat in my freezer! I survived, but it could have been so much better! I hadn't wasted my resources, but by not using all that I had, my survival was not what it could have been.

Just as I failed to use all of my nutritional resources, the church often fails to use all of the spiritual gifts available to it. My failure was due to ignorance, but the failure of the church is often due to racism.

How much talent do we have sitting in our pews that we are not using because of our racial bias? Are there individuals in your church or in your neighborhood who are not considered for particular jobs because societal norms deny responsibility to those individuals? I have a feeling that if we are honest, we know of situations where there are individuals who are being denied the opportunity to fully serve the church because of the bias, be it racial or otherwise, that is facing them. To be a Christian is to confront the evil of that bias so that such individuals can give to the church all the gifts and talents with which the Lord has blessed them.

This is that sin of stereotyping again. It is hard to think of a personal sin that has received as little attention as this one. We seem content to let it cheat us out of the resources that God intends the church to have. I wonder why we are satisfied with such a sterile existence. Should the church merely survive? Or should we fulfill our potential by using all of the resources the Lord has put at our disposal? To do this we must take off the blinders that this society has placed on our eyes and use the eyes that the Lord has given us. The criteria that we use to determine how an individual can best serve the church must never deviate from a scriptural standard laid out by the Bible. And we must confront those who continue to believe this society's lies about tracking of ethnic and racial minorities. We must help turn some of our fellow church members to the Lord to be freed of such biases.

17

The Bird

> If therefore you are presenting your offering at the altar, and there
> remember that your brother has something against you, leave your
> offering there before the altar, and go your way; first be reconciled
> to your brother, and then come and present your offering.
>
> Matthew 5:23–24

There is a story of a little girl who loved animals. She often brought them home and cared for them. Her room was always filled with various rodents, insects, and other small creatures that she kept as pets. Often her parents would have to force her to set many of her animal friends free because the room simply could not hold them all. Although she truly liked all animals, it was the smaller and weaker animals that often captured her heart. Her parents lost count of the number of times she brought home a sick or wounded animal and nursed that creature back to health.

One day while she was in the woods, she saw some boys that she knew hurling stones at a tree. She walked over to greet them but to her horror she quickly learned that the target of their stones was a small bird. It was injured and unable to fly. She rushed to the boys and began yelling at them to stop. However, the boys merely laughed and continued their game. When yelling failed to stop the boys, she jumped in the way between them and the bird. In anger they shoved her aside and continued their sport. Undaunted she interfered with them repeatedly. Each time, the boys would shove her aside or knock her down in order to get a good shot at their target. This continued for several minutes until finally a stone knocked the bird to the ground.

The boys cheered their success and gathered about the fallen creature. The bird was wounded but not dead. So the boys began to prod the bird with sticks. Once again the girl began to cry and scolded the boys. She tried to protect the bird, but the boys just pushed her away. Finally, though, they tired of their game and began to walk away.

Eager to care for the animal, the compassionate girl reached for the fallen creature. However, to her shock and to the delight of the boys, the bird seized her hand with its beak, squeezing until it drew blood. The boys roared with laughter. Embarrassed and hurt, the girl jumped away, her hand throbbing from the bite and her pride crushed by the laughter of her peers. Scornfully, they told the girl that she should have let them finish the bird off. If she had left them alone, she could have saved herself a bit of pain and humiliation from an ungrateful animal.

Should we be surprised by the reaction of the bird? Probably not, if we can look at life from its viewpoint. Imagine for a moment that you are this bird. You are sitting up in a tree just minding your own business. Suddenly a group of these large creatures comes by and tries to harm you with rocks and to mock you. You try to get away but these brutes will not leave you alone. Another one of these vile creatures comes by and makes more noise than all the rest. Suddenly one of the rocks knocks you unconscious to the ground. You wake up terrifed to see these creatures surrounding you. They continue to abuse you by poking you with huge pieces of wood. You lunge at your tormentors but to no avail. They are able to keep out of the way of your only weapon, your beak. Finally you think the torment has stopped. But then one of these big creatures reaches down to you again. It has no weapon but both of its hands are heading straight for your body.

What would be your response? Seen from the perspective of the bird, you have no way of knowing that this last creature has good intentions. All you have known is torment from these creatures. You expect more torment and attack your potential benefactor.

Often when white Americans attempt to reach out to those they have previously shunned, they are dismayed when African Americans are not eager to greet them with enthusiasm and gratefulness. Instead they are often met with suspicion and bitterness. Discouraged by what they perceive as a lack of gratitude, whites then are likely to withdraw back into their own world and dismiss blacks as ungrateful clods.

If one is willing to think about the plight of blacks in this country, one might not be surprised by such a response. African Americans are often reacting out of a past pain instead of a present reality. This reaction is as rational as the bird's reaction to the girl. The natural response to continued abuse is a developing mistrust of the abusive person. History clearly shows that African Americans have suffered continued abuse from whites and will often not be eager to trust whites, even those who are reaching out to them.

Even if most of African Americans today are like me and have not lived through the horrors of the overt racism of Jim Crow laws and the terror of lynchings, we have heard of these things from our parents and grand-parents. We have read about them in our history books. We have seen the historical effects of these social phenomena in our communities. Yet many blacks, angered by all of this, have never had even one white per-son state that they are sorry for all that has happened to them. Or it has been qualified by a comment such as "Those things were terrible in the past. I am glad that everything is good today."

For such African Americans to begin to work toward a plan of recon-ciliation, there will have to be white individuals in their lives who truly attempt to understand the injustices that black Americans have faced and continue to face, people who express true regret and are committed to helping America overcome the sickness of racism. Anything less than this will be seen for the shallow and empty commitment to reconciliation that it is, and the bird will continue to bite back.

Those with a shallow commitment to reconciliation between the races will not understand this reaction and resent it. They will quickly be dis-couraged in their attempts to reach out. A deep commitment to recon-ciliation is needed to endure the potential rebuffs and lack of respon-siveness from blacks. Those who are deeply committed will continue to work to gain the trust of those who have been wronged. At times indi-viduals with this deep commitment will understand what is happening and allow minorities to feel the natural pain of past injustices. At other times they will be our friends who will confront us with the wrong of our distrustful attitudes. In both situations we must let love, not some misplaced guilt or a power trip, determine which is the proper action. When reaching out is done in love, eventually even the most hardened and bitter African American may have his or her heart melted by the uncompromising love of our Lord.

18

The Other

Those who need the gospel message of hope and the reality of love, don't get it, and the isolated church keeps evangelizing the same people over and over until its only mission finally is to entertain itself.

Charles Colson
Loving God

One of the great American rituals is for young people to get their wits scared out of them through some horror movie. Some of the horror movies of the '50s and '60s look pretty corny to me. I was weaned on movies such as *Halloween* and *The Thing*. I guess today's youths are getting their frights from the *Nightmare on Elm Street* series. Very few of these movies are well done and most are not exactly edifying to our Christian walk. However, one must admit that the Hollywood directors who created these movies have figured out one thing: the creepier the monster, the better the scare.

When the villain is some inhuman creature, it's scary because we don't know what the monster is capable of. This uncertainty cannot help but add to the fright.

This same fear of the unknown may be what causes us to be apprehensive when encountering strangers. We do not know what this person is like and thus we don't know what to expect from him.

This fear makes a certain phenomenon in race relations all the more disturbing. This is the tendency to see different races as "the other." We often react to people of different races as though they were inhuman creatures. We tend to hone in on any physical dissimilarity and allow that to foster our image of other races as being categorically different from the rest of us. Thus we do not believe that it's possible to

87

relate to them or that they would be able to understand us. They are "the other."

It's natural to choose friends who are most like us. In many respects this is good. It is good to have friends who share the same interests, goals, and beliefs that we do. However, we take this a step too far when our friends must have the same race as well. There should be no inherent estrangement between white, black, brown, and yellow people, especially Christians. Any racial separation that we allow in the church is based on social tradition or personal inadequacies rather than on spiritual incompatibility. Intellectually we would deny that we separate ourselves on the basis of race. However, reality often shows us that this is the case. We assume that the individuals of those different races have different interests than we do, so we never get close enough to discover if we do indeed have things in common.

It is true that I have more in common with another black man than I do with a white man. Blacks share a history and a place in American culture that is unique among the races. However, I have more in common with a Christian than I do with a non-Christian. So who do I have more in common with: a black non-Christian or a white Christian? It is not even close. I share the same common purpose of life with my Christian friends. I share the same source of love and acceptance. I have access to the same avenue of freedom. In fact in all of the important questions concerning life, purpose, and significance, I am in agreement with Christians of every race and nationality. In all of our basic needs and desires we look to the same source. With my black friends the similar cultural background is important in certain ways in my life, but this similarity pales in significance when I look at the similarities I share with growing Christians.

I am not advocating that one completely overlook the importance of racial background. Different cultural backgrounds can bring some misunderstandings to interracial encounters. And it is important to keep in touch with one's roots. However, we must not forsake the opportunity to reach out and minister to others, just to maintain cultural or racial purity. In fact part of the joy of relationships should be learning to cope with the differences and having the chance to learn from them. We must learn to celebrate our differences as well as our similarities. We cheat ourselves if we do not take the opportunity to develop friends of different races.

As Christians we can gain the opportunity to minister to others if we can overlook differences and concentrate on the similar needs that we all have. We humans are a lot more alike than we often care to admit. We all want to find purpose in life that is greater than ourselves. We all need relationships to feel that we are accepted and loved for who we are, not for what we can do. We all desire to know what is the right thing to do and to have the strength to do it (see Romans 7:15–20). In this world we use psychology, philosophy, and reason to try to meet these needs, but they can give only partial answers. The final answer can be found only in the lordship of Christ. We Christians can offer this answer to anyone who is willing to accept it, if we are willing to accept that person as one of us and not as "the other." Unfortunately, we do not always do this.

I have a Hispanic friend who told me a story about her father's experience at a white church. He was not a regular churchgoer but he went to a couple of church activities out of curiosity. In those activities the men of the church tended to show only shallow kindness to him before going on to their real friends. Once they ignored him altogether, leaving him at the church alone while they went to have breakfast together. I have to wonder if they would have done this if he were white. If he were white, they may have still been uncomfortable with him, as we are with any new acquaintance, but would they not have tried to include him in their activities? Obviously he stopped going to the church. He was the other. He was tolerated but not really accepted.

Unfortunately most minorities have had experiences like this one. We visit a white church and people are kind, but everyone seems a little nervous around us. Or they may try to act black. They act as if it is a supreme effort to relate to us. We are perceived as different, the other. But why? I may be black but I have many of the same concerns that my white friends have, concerns about my job, money, and relationships. It is true that being black has shaped me in ways that my white friends have not been shaped. But I am more like my white friends than different from them.

We as Christians would do well to remember that the church is in a war. In a spiritual war, as in a physical one, we don't have time to focus on petty differences. When we were fighting Desert Storm in Iraq, men and women from different races and nationalities united to fight a common foe. There was no time for racism then. They were relying on each other to get safely through the war.

We Christians need to rely on each other. We cannot afford to consider anyone as the other. We are all on the same side fighting Satan, a foe who is bigger than all of us. We have an ally, however, who is greater than our foe—our Lord Jesus Christ. I believe that one of the ways that Christ is going to help us win the battle is by pulling us together. In that way we will not only win the war but also discover the joy of working with each other.

Acceptance
at the Most Intimate Level

There is one body and one Spirit, just as also you were called in one
hope of your calling.

Ephesians 4:4

The acceptance of interracial dating and marriage has served as
a significant indicator of the level of acceptance different races have for
each other. To reject interracial marriage implies a rejection of other races
whether we want to accept that fact or not. Jeanette Davidson argues that
society's barriers to interracial marriages imply it is possible to group
people into exclusive racial groups. This grouping can imply the existence of a racial hierarchy. Of course in this hierarchy, blacks can be
placed at the bottom and thus can be seen as the lowest form of
humankind.[1] Therefore individuals may seem justified in rejecting those
of other races in non-romantic areas of life as well.

Walter Wangerin tells the story of his three-year-old adopted black
son who is denied the friendship of a three-year-old white girl. The reasoning of the girl's mother is simple. Interracial relationships may lead to
marriage. By denying her daughter the opportunity to develop interracial relationships she will protect the girl from the danger of an interracial marriage down the road.[2] The mother has a point. If you allow individuals of the opposite sex to become friends, then the possibility of them
falling in love becomes a reality. If we ban interracial marriages, we must
ban interracial friendships as well.

I have a black friend who told me the following story. When he was
younger he became friends with a white girl in his youth group. He often

had dinner with her family and quickly became friends with members of that family. However, as his friendship with the girl deepened, he began to notice a difference in the way the family treated him. As soon as the specter of a possible romantic interest began to develop, the relationship with the family became decidedly colder. The family began to erect barriers to prevent the friendship from going any further. They made it clear that race relations can develop only to a certain extent. They effectively ended the friendship between my friend and any members of the family. This resulted in my friend's loss of respect for that family and the end to any racial reconciliation.

Society Determines Morality

Often I hear that it is okay for Christians to reject interracial dating and marriage because society is not yet ready for them. This is disturbing, since it means that Christians are now looking to society to determine our morality rather than the church helping to shape society's morality. This has led to disturbing situations. I have known Christian parents who have allowed their children to date non-Christians and yet would not allow them to date people of another race. This implies that one must consider race more than spiritual growth in choosing a mate. Shouldn't Christians have a different value system than this? It seems that we are more afraid of societal stigma than justice. As Christians we emphasize the inner person rather than the outer characteristics, except when it comes to race. When it comes to racial issues, Christians often bow to society and set their values and morality aside. Our pastors often teach us that our desire to conform to this culture's values will lead us into sin. This is one of those areas where we are easily led.

Christians must develop morality apart from society, on this as well as other issues. If we do not do so, then society dictates to us what is right and wrong. If society should decide that blacks are pieces of property, as they did at one time in our history, or if society should decide that blacks do not deserve political representation, as was the case in South Africa, should Christians go along with these policies in an effort to conform to society?

Whether we want to believe it or not, whenever we do not accept interracial relationships between the sexes, we are part of the problem in race relations. If we take the position that racial segregation is acceptable in marriage, then we have to accept that segregation in all areas of life is okay. This concerns me. The same reasoning that supports segregated marriage can support other types of segregation that may be more oppressive. This has been true historically. The fear of interracial marriage has been used to justify segregation in the workplace, in housing, in schools. This in turn fosters a white superiority ideology.

Protection against interracial marriage was part of the justification for Jim Crow laws. Earlier in this century when individuals fought for racial equality but were afraid to support interracial marriages, their philosophy was suspect. Gordon Allport gives an example of this:

> When a person with a strong anti-Negro bias is confronted with evidence favorable to the Negro he frequently pops up with the well-known matrimonial question: "Would you want your sister to marry a Negro?" . . . As soon as the interlocutor says, "No," or hesitates in his reply, the biased person can say in effect, "See, there just *is* something different and impossible about the Negro," or "I was right all along—for the Negro has an objectionable essence in his nature" [author's emphasis].[3]

The racist gains justification for his or her position because the integrationist is unwilling to confront all barriers erected against integration. If we are committed to creating a diverse society, we will refuse to reject the involvement of any other racial or ethnic group at any level. We cannot fully accept minorities into our neighborhoods or occupations until we are willing to accept the possibility that they may come into our families. Whenever racial acceptance is complete, blacks and whites will be able to intermarry as easily as Italians and Irish. The church needs to be part of the process that will bring the races to that point.

The Church's Stand

Many in the church need to rethink their beliefs about the legitimacy of interracial dating and marriage. In light of the fact that there is no solid scriptural basis for opposing it, we should ask what the church's stance should be concerning interracial dating. This stance has very practical implications. For the most part the church is silent concerning this issue. But this silence is often interpreted as assent to the condemnation of interracial dating. We in the church need to think through the racist implications of such a stance. It implies that it is perfectly fine to assess negative value to an individual simply because of his or her race when

93

attempting to decide whether that person is a suitable mate for one's friends or offspring. We have then opened a door by which the aversive racism of many church members can manifest itself. Then it is fair to ask, do we deplore racism or do we condone it?

I do not believe that the Lord is calling all Christians to be involved in interracial romantic relationships. That kind of symbolic action only produces weak relationships that founder when difficulties come. Many people are not suited for interracial marriage because they would not be able to face society's disapproval of such relationships. I do believe, however, that the Lord has called all of us to accept such relationships when we find them. Race should not be a factor in our evaluation of any relationship. While we have the right to decide whether or not we personally will engage in an interracial relationship, we do not have the right to decide that for our friends or family members.

If the acceptance of interracial marriage is a significant test of racial tolerance, then clearly we must work to bring about racial reconciliation before these relationships will be completely accepted in our society. Racial reconciliation offers us freedom from the limits that racism has placed on us. We can be free to love whomever we meet as deeply as the Lord will allow us, without regard to race. And the opportunity to love must constantly be the great motivator for Christians.

20

The Bible
and Interracial Marriage

> Beware of the false prophets, who come to you in sheep's clothing,
> but inwardly are ravenous wolves. You will know them by their fruits.
>
> Matthew 7:15–16

In 1982 a controversy developed in a small evangelical school in South Carolina. This school was Bob Jones University, and the controversy surrounded the fact that students going to that school would no longer be able to receive any federal financial aid. The aid was denied because the school was accused of practicing discrimination. It forbade interracial dating. The president of the school insisted that this was not a racist practice. He stated:

> We believe that God made races as they are. He made black people. He made yellow people. He made white people. We believe God intends for those distinctions to remain. That's not racist.[1]

His scriptural support for this position lies in Acts 17:26. In this passage Paul talks about the fact that the Lord has sovereignly determined the places of all the nations but that all nations are of "one blood." This justification of a ban of interracial dating relies on the fact that God obviously made us different. The racial difference is part of his plan. Therefore if we ruin this difference by distorting the distinctions that the Lord himself has given us, we are in disobedience to him. In short, the way things are is the way things are supposed to be.

Scriptures in the Old Testament are also used to show how interracial relationships are out of the will of God.[2] In many of those passages God

95

forbids the Israelites to intermarry with other nations. The Lord is explicit in telling his children that to do so would court disaster. Instead of being able to conquer their enemies, their enemies would be able to conquer them. People use these verses to show the seriousness that the Lord apparently attaches to this sin of interracial marriage. They assert that its importance would mean that it's not just a commandment for that particular time but that it is relevant in today's circumstances as well. In other words, this is not like some mere cultural dietary law that we can overlook today. It's a sin that had a direct tie to the failure of Israel as a nation. Thus it must be a universal truth that transcends cultural boundaries.

Before we believe that the Bible rejects interracial relationships we better take a careful look at the Scriptures. I realize that there may be more arguments that are used to justify racial separation than I will deal with here. Most of these arguments tend to imply a white superiority (such as the curse of Ham) that most people reject today. I will deal with the two I have heard that are not overtly racist, even though I believe that these arguments are seriously flawed.

God's Purpose for the Nations

An honest study of the Bible reveals the weaknesses of the first argument. This particular interpretation of Acts 17:26 is argumentative at best. Probably a better interpretation would be that Paul is showing the authority of the Lord to place nations where he chooses. In this passage Paul is evangelizing individuals who are polytheistic and so he is trying to show that one God is responsible for all that we see. He is not insisting that God made the nations the way they are in order to preserve some sort of racial purity. In fact, part of the verse talks about how we are of the same blood. This seems to indirectly state that distinctions such as race are really unimportant to the Lord. To interpret the verse as God's directive to keep the races separated is to rip it completely out of context in an effort to justify a specific stand.

Do we as Christians believe that everything is the way it is because God wanted it to be that way? God has a permissive will that should not be confused with his perfect will. He allows things to happen but that doesn't mean he wants them to happen. Was the needless slaughter of six million Jews in World War II part of God's will? He certainly permitted it. We can probably find some fanatical religious fringe group that believes that this is God's punishment on the Jews for crimes against Christ, but most evangelicals do not believe that this was part of God's perfect will. Everything we know about the character of the Lord tells us that such acts are an insult to him. He may permit them because of our freedom and the wickedness of our hearts, but do not mistake that for an endorsement.

Therefore, I would argue that the presence of many nations may be part of God's permissive will but not his perfect will. The existence of many nations does not imply a condemnation of interracial unions. Rather, it seems to me that the reconciling nature of our Lord would mean that interracial unions are part of his perfect will.

Do mere physical differences imply some will of our Lord? Because there are definite physical distinctions between the races, does this mean that God intended that the races should be forever separated? If one follows this logic, then it must be permissible for men to physically beat their wives. After all, we know that men are stronger than women. The Lord must have given men this strength for a reason. Perhaps we can begin to see the danger of inferring God's will from factors of physical difference. We discover God's will from an honest interpretation of his Word and from knowledge of his character. This means laying aside our own preconceptions, studying his Word, and spending time with him. It means taking great care not to introduce our own cultural standards into our interpretation of his will.

Prohibition of Intermarriage

When dealing with the second argument concerning the Lord's prohibiting Israel from marrying people from other nations, we again must interpret the Scripture in its proper context. It is true that there were severe consequences for those who took wives from other nations. The reason for God's command, however, was not because God was prohibiting mixing of the races but because the people of other nations didn't know Yahweh. In 1 Kings 11:2 God gives the reason for his directive: "for they will surely turn your heart away after their gods."

Most of the passages that prohibit taking wives from other nations explicitly point out that the reason is the foreign religion that such wives would introduce to the society.[3] In fact many of the passages go on to state that the downfall of the individuals who transgress in this way would be due to the fact that they would begin to follow the gods of their spouses instead of the one true God. Solomon is a good example of this. God is not trying to avoid having an impure race but rather an impure faith.

97

What does this mean to twentieth-century America? It is important to remember that in biblical times nations were more culturally identified with their gods than we are today. To marry into another race then was to marry into another religion. This is not the case today. Christianity has grown to where it transcends race in our country. If the sin is to marry someone who may pull you from your faith, then I can infer this universal principle from these passages: Do not marry a non-Christian. For a black Christian man, marriage to a black woman who is not a Christian is sin, but marriage to a white woman who is a Christian is not. Ultimately, if one is honest, one must come to the conclusion that the Scriptures are silent concerning the sinfulness of interracial marriages if both individuals are believers. We must find a different criterion if we are to condemn this practice.

Justifying Racism

If the arguments against interracial relationships are so weak, then it makes sense to ask why a significant number of Christians accept these arguments. I believe that modern Christians sometimes accept such weak arguments for the same reason that many white supremacists use the Scriptures to justify their racist ideology. In both cases, individuals are using the Bible to legitimate cultural attitudes, even though they are not consistent with the spirit of the Bible. It is incredible how easily we can ignore verses that discuss how the Lord has created us equal, so that we can justify our hatreds and fears (see Gal. 3:28; Acts 10:34–35; Rom. 3:9). I have found that individuals from all parts of society—black and white, liberal and conservative, poor and rich—tend to bend the Word of God in such a way as to justify their own shortcomings. This blindness is the natural outcome of our attempts to hide from our sins.

Interracial marriage has not yet received full support in our society. Therefore it's safe for the aversive racist to oppose such relationships. There are many fine Christians who seem to be tolerant of other races, even to the point of ministering to them, and yet they would resist their children marrying interracially. They may think their views have the backing of Scripture but in reality they are being influenced by their own racism. Instead of using Scripture to disclose their sins they use it to hide their sins. It is heresy in its most potent form.

It's painful for Christians to admit to sin in their lives. However, Christian growth consists of recognizing sin and then committing that area of one's life to the Lord. This must be done with the sin of racism. What repentance is truly about is acknowledging the ways in which we try to justify our behavior, and then renouncing those ways so that our Lord can clean up the mess that we have made in our lives.

The degree of acceptance of interracial marriage in a community is an indicator of the degree of acceptance of minority individuals in a community. Resistance to interracial marriage in the Christian church tells us that we have hidden from the reality of the sin of racism for too long. Honest repentance should then be in order. That should not frighten us, because honest repentance is at the center of what being a Christian is all about.

21

What about the Children?

> The cross between a white man and an Indian is an Indian; the cross between a white man and a Negro is a Negro; the cross between a white man and a Hindu is a Hindu; and the cross between any of the three European races and a Jew is a Jew.
>
> Madison Grant
> *The Passing of the Great Race*

Anyone who becomes involved in an interracial romantic relationship eventually hears *the question*. Those who oppose interracial marriage may ask it like this: "Well it's okay if you want to take on the stigma that society offers but have you thought about the children?" Let's look at the facts and the fiction that surround this topic.

There seems to be a general belief that the children produced by interracial relationships will suffer harm. First, some argue that the children will be teased and treated cruelly by their peers. Second, some individuals fear that such children will suffer from confusion because they will lack a pure racial identity, and the world will refuse to accept them. Because of these problems the children may come to resent the parents for bringing them into the world. Let me take these arguments one at a time.

The possibility that these children will be horribly teased may be true. Children need little encouragement to mock each other, and a light-skinned child having one black parent and one white parent would provide sufficient fodder. We all know that a child who is different in any way will be teased. Children are masterful at finding some aspect of a weaker child to pick on, and there are no guarantees that the child of same race parents will not be teased.

100

The important thing is that a child feel good about himself regardless of his external characteristics. This self-confidence goes a long way in turning away mockery. It seems to me that the most important way any parent can protect his or her child from ridicule is to give the child a sense of confidence and self-worth that a loving family can provide.

I have spoken with an elementary school teacher who has taught many children from mixed marriages. She has confirmed my suspicions that the internal personality of the child is more important to the adjustment of the child to school and peers than his or her racial makeup.

Evidence from the experience of many interracial families today reveals that children from these families do not suffer teasing because of their race. This is probably due to the lack of stigma attached to being biracial. The disproportionate teasing of biracial children is a myth. It may have happened at one point in our history. It may be true in certain limited areas of the nation, but I do not believe it to be true any longer in most of this nation.

The second argument is that such children will suffer from an identity crisis. In a black–white marriage such children will not know if they are black or if they are white. Where will they find their identity? There have been some studies that show slight identity conflict among biracial children.[1] However, these studies show that the children still maintain a highly realistic perception of themselves. In other words, they seem to be very aware of their particular situation as a biracial child as well as the strengths and drawbacks that are associated with this situation. These studies show that often the children tend to be happy with their dual heritage, feeling that it gives them the best of both worlds. A separate study has found no negative effects of children living in a biracial environment. In fact, it states that they seem to enjoy certain advantages over children who have parents of the same race: mastery of a second language, ability to enjoy the dominant culture, and a tendency to have more relationships with people from varied racial groups.[2] Because there are so few studies that have been done, there is no assurance that there is no serious negative effect of interracial unions on children. However, the evidence so far points more to the benefits rather than the drawbacks of being biracial.

This racial identity argument bothers me. It seems to imply that we are looking for our identity in our racial background. I look for mine in my relationship with my Lord. That is more important to me than my being black. I would not marry a woman who finds her racial background more important than her spiritual background. Furthermore, if I have children, I want to teach them that their identity and self-worth depend on their being children of God. I hope that we as Christians have gotten beyond looking at race as being so important that if we are not sure what our racial background is, we do not feel that we can be whole.

The importance that we attach to a racial identity not only shows how important the socially constructed concept of race is in our culture, but also reveals how much we adhere to a belief in racial purity. We may actually begin to think that most of us are 100 percent racially pure. The whole idea that there can be racial purity is another myth that we should deflate. In fact racial purity is becoming increasingly rare in our country, if it ever truly existed. It has been stated that the average black American has 25 percent traceable white genes and the average white American has 5 percent traceable black genes.[3] I have Indian and Irish blood in me. So why do I not suffer an identity crisis over whether I am black, Indian, or Irish? In our multicultural society the trend of mixing the races will grow. Since there are so few people of pure race left, why should we feel that such purity is necessary or even desirable for sound mental health? Those who emphasize the importance of racial purity create unnecessary problems for biracial individuals. Ideally, as we create a society that deemphasizes racial differences, the need of biracial individuals to struggle with identity will be less.

When we are asking about the children, I think that often we are asking how we can categorize those individuals by their race. For this reason biracial children become a threat to the prevailing racial system in our society. This aspect alone may explain why interracial marriage is such a concern to many racist organizations. It also illustrates the importance that race still plays in determining the place and status of individuals in our society. It seems to me that when our identity is based more on our relationship with Christ and less on our physical characteristics, we will have much less of a struggle accepting biracial individuals. Thus it is the job of the church to do all that is needed for biracial individuals to experience total acceptance.

When two Christians marry, they have a similar background no matter what their racial cultures may be. All marriage partners have differences, be they racial or otherwise, that must be dealt with, but the foundation of the relationship, if it is to be successful, must be in Christ. All Christian marriages should be based on a shared faith. When this is true then the children benefit. To the degree that we perceive biracial Christian couples as having less in common than same race couples who do not share the same faith, we reveal that we have accepted society's standards rather than our Lord's for what makes a successful marriage. And to the degree that we believe that biracial Christian children are worse off than same race Christian children, we cheapen our Christian faith.

PART 3

the
NARROW PATH

Don't you just love the imagery that is given to us in the Bible? In discussing salvation, Jesus tells us that it is a narrow path behind a narrow gate. He could have just talked about the narrow gate but he didn't. I think this was intentional.

If salvation were just a narrow gate, it would imply that we make a decision for salvation and then we are done with it. In reality, though, we must also walk down the narrow path. We know that salvation is more than a onetime decision. It also involves a lifelong promise of sanctification where we gain the opportunity to become more like our Savior. It's not works that are needed for salvation, but rather the changes in our lives that reveal our new spiritual condition. I think this is what James is talking about when he says, "I will show you my faith by my works" (James 2:18).

Both the gate and the path are narrow. Once we make a decision for salvation, we walk down the path of sanctification by making similar decisions the rest of our lives. Salvation is a decision to surrender our lives to the Lord.

Sanctification is a result of spiritual growth that comes when we surrender more and more intimate parts of our lives to the Lord. A Christian who makes only the initial decision of salvation never grows very much and is similar to one who starts out on a path and then stops just inside the gate. That person may be "safe" on the path but can never enjoy the fruits that lie farther down the road. Having gained spiritual salvation but not spiritual empowerment, such individuals often resemble those who stand just outside the gate and they are not able to make much of an influence for the Lord's kingdom.

Dealing with racism is similar. A decision of forgiveness or repentance is only a starting point. Recognizing many of the problems that racism has created in our society takes us a little farther down the path. To get all the way down, however, we are going to have to fashion new solutions to this old problem. We will have to find ways to live out new principles if we are to achieve the sort of racial harmony that our Lord wants for us. To fail to do so will leave us just inside the gate, recognizing that reconciliation is needed but unable to push the process any further along. If we desire to see the races come together under the umbrella of our faith, we cannot be content with merely entering the gate but we must work together to help each other move down the path.

22

Can Christianity and Racism Mix?

> There is a way which seems right to a man,
> But its end is the way of death.
>   Proverbs 14:12

When Christianity is used to promote the social desires of its adherents, it may be used to hold down the underprivileged. Christianity in the pure "love your neighbor" form will completely alter the institutions that would denigrate others. In its past, the Christian church has done both. It was instrumental in addressing the evils of slavery and in bringing women the vote. The church has also served to justify systems of white supremacy and oppression of women. Understanding the justifications for racial equality that are found in Christianity will enable us to use our faith to guarantee racial justice.

I am often surrounded by well-meaning and well-educated individuals who believe that a secular philosophy of humanism is the best way to find such justice. I have honestly struggled with the possibility that they may be right, but I have come to the conclusion that they are not. This chapter is a result of my struggle. I hope that it may provide some intellectual fuel for Christians who, like me, have to deal with supporters of humanism on a regular basis.

Worldview of Racism

We need to make an honest assessment of the compatibility of the worldview of Christianity and the worldview of racism. What is a racist view of the world? It is that the worth of an individual is based on the physical and racial characteristics of that individual. We assign different values to different animal species according to physical differences. A dog is seen as more valuable than an ant, and a man is more valuable than either. Because of physical differences different animal species are capable of different tasks and different levels of reasoning.

It is obvious that there are differences between blacks, whites, Indians, and Hispanics. Who is to say that skin difference is not representative of different levels of abilities in each? The stereotype of blacks is that they are physically superior but mentally inferior to whites. If the racist who holds this view is right, then blacks can excel only in the physical dimension of society. Blacks, therefore, should not be given opportunities to achieve in the social, intellectual, and emotional arenas where others excel because blacks are not as capable of handling those dimensions. The argument continues that diverting resources from the majority of intelligent white citizens to give minorities a chance is inefficient. Minority groups will ultimately benefit when resources are kept in the white community because then whites will be free to apply their superior talents to make society a better place.

This viewpoint used to sound absurd—until books like *The Bell Curve* revealed that the adoption of such a viewpoint is not impossible, even in our "enlightened" society.[1] The authors of this book justify allocating fewer resources to minorities since, on average, their scores on IQ tests are lower than those of whites. One should realize that this racial-difference theory is impossible to scientifically refute. Many have tried by pointing out that institutional barriers—such as inferior educational facilities—have prevented minorities from succeeding. Others have proposed the "culture of poverty" theory. It says that since minorities are more likely to be born into a poor subculture, they are more likely to be taught fatalism and other personal characteristics that tend to discourage them from trying to succeed and escape the poverty that they were born into.

Analysis that tries to take into account these and other factors that contribute to poverty is incomplete. First of all, subjective attitudes such as fatalism are impossible to adequately measure. We may not know if minorities are truly more fatalistic than whites, and if they are to what degree they are fatalistic. Also, the cultural measurements that have been used have failed to completely explain the income differential between the races. It is the nature of a statistical test to leave unexplained some proportion of the differences that are found between two groups. Because we cannot infer a completely cultural explanation, the possibility of a physical or racial dimension remains.

Worldview of Christianity

The argument for white superiority can be refuted if we change the way we assign value to human beings. If we assign value to human beings simply on the basis of their being human and not because of any innate abilities, then all human beings are of equal value and the racist point of view is refuted. Keith Roberts asserts that Christianity does this. He notes that it is not an accident that the official stand of all major Christian denominations in the United States condemns racism.[2]

How does Christianity evaluate individuals? All are evaluated according to the spiritual relationship that they have with God. In Christianity such a relationship is available to anyone, so there is no partiality. Everyone, from the dullest imbecile to the most creative genius, is able to gain this relationship through Christ's sacrifice. Therefore, a true Christian should never look down on any other human being, because each person is one for whom the Lord died.

The amazing thing about Christianity is that it protects equality every step of the way. First, the Bible says that everyone has sinned (Rom. 3:23). What does that mean? In the Old Testament, one of the words that is used to define sin means "to miss" (see 1 Samuel 19:4 and 1 Kings 22:52). Thus to sin means to miss the mark that God has set for us. God has a mark for our lives that he wants us to make. But we all choose our own path. We want to be free from the laws of God to decide our own destiny and the ability to determine the morality of others. It is not only that I do not want to steal, I also do not want others to have the right to steal. Thus I desire to set the standard and the mark for everyone. I want to be God. To the degree that anyone erases God's mark, strives for self-determination, and decides his own morality to replace God's morality, that person has sinned. The Bible says that I have sinned and you have sinned. All have sinned. We have equality.

Second, the Bible assures us that everyone needs to be redeemed from sin (Rom. 3:10). As long as we keep a sin nature we will continue to rebel against God. We need this nature changed if we are to stop rebelling against God and to work with him so that we may find the mark that he has set for us. We cannot find this mark on our own for it is against our very nature to seek it. We need the outside help that only a pure and loving Lord can give. I need help and you need help. We all need help. We have equality.

The provision the Lord has given so that we will have the help we need is a provision given to all of us (John 1:12). It was a single historical event: the death and resurrection of Jesus Christ. There is nothing that anyone ever did to deserve God's sending his Son to come down and die for us. None of us are good enough to demand that. The idea of God sacrificing his Son for humans is similar to a man sacrificing his son to save an anthill. The only major difference is that our worth cannot even be compared to that of Jesus. He is much farther above us than we are above ants. One of the major ways that we determine the worth of an object is by assessing the price for which that item would be bought. God bought our salvation with the life of his Son. That is how much each of us is worth to him. As incredible as it may seem, my value is worth the life of the Son of my Creator. God sacrificed his Son for each of us, so the value of each of us is the same. We have equality.

To be a Christian is to assign infinite worth to each individual. When you do that, you can see that the value distinctions of race, ethnicity, and gender are cheap and shallow.

It is intellectually impossible to adopt a racist worldview and a Christian worldview at the same time. To adopt the former is to seek ways to value one group above another on the basis of race. To adopt the latter is to realize that all have infinite worth and potential. Adopting the latter means that any physical difference between us is meaningless. Thus to see the world through the eyes of God renders justification for racial prejudice meaningless.

Ethical Relativism

Because reconciliation is a spiritual concept and not a political one, secular philosophies, such as humanism, have only a limited ability to make it a reality. Martin Luther King believed that liberal secular organizations were beneficial to the cause of civil rights but they were not sufficient to bring about reconciliation. Such organizations rely on reason and humanity to justify the stances that they take on subjects such as racism. These motivations, King asserted, are not sufficient because they do not take into consideration the evil and selfishness that reside within our hearts.[3]

The real problem lies in the philosophies that drive these groups. The general philosophy of organizations such as the American Civil Liberties

Union (ACLU) is one of ethical relativism. One does not have to be an atheist or an agnostic to buy into this philosophy (although that is extremely helpful). One does have to believe, however, that if there is a God, his effect on our lives is so remote that it is up to us humans to look out for ourselves. God's influence in the real world, then, is not very important compared to the influence of our own decisions and actions.

Ethical relativism asserts that we humans are intellectual beings who must set our own standards. No one else should decide what we need in our lives. If we can gain all of the relevant facts about a subject, then as intelligent and rational beings we will be able to make the proper decision for our lives. The only restriction that should be placed on our actions is when those actions interfere with the possible happiness of others. These restrictions become societal laws. In a democratic and just society, they are determined by general consensus. Thus a society picks laws that best suit the needs for that particular society. Morality on an individual and a societal level will be relative to the needs of that individual and of society.

For the proper morality of a society to be developed, all individuals in society must be free to choose their direction in life. Racism inhibits the options available to members of the minority classes. Therefore racism is immoral in a humanistic society because it is detrimental to the ability of individuals to choose their own path in life. All individuals must be free to fully participate in whatever activities their personal morality will allow.

There are, however, contradictions within this argument that allow for the legitimization of racism. One problem is the very notion that morality can be relative. Once morality is relative, then anything is possible. We lose the ability to determine that something is morally wrong. Thus the racist is able to state to the ethical relativist: "Advocating racial justice is fine for you, but I as a rational human being have chosen to have none of it in my life." We all know hateful individuals who are rational people. They are not mentally disturbed but they harbor deep hatred for certain groups or individuals. If these people are racists, ethical relativism justifies that racism because they have chosen their own system of morality.

This brings up the dilemma of rational thought. Rationality is a myth. No one can be completely objective. All of us have allowed emotions and biases to interfere with decision making. We expect that people will

111

often make important decisions because of a feeling in the gut. Intelligent rationality has nothing, or at least very little, to do with it. Therefore the relativist argument that we can develop some sort of rational morality depends on an ability to be completely rational, and we are not capable of that.

The relativist will answer that relativism sets moral limits. Those limits come into play when the morality of certain individuals affects the lives of other individuals. Therefore, while a person may be free to hold racist attitudes, to act out of those attitudes is immoral since it would negatively affect the lives of other human beings. There are two problems with this position.

The first problem is that external actions are regulated while leaving the internal man untouched. It assumes that internal, personal philosophy can be kept from affecting external acts. This has not proven to be true. We tend to seek opportunities to act out externally what we believe internally. Thus if the racial hatred of the inner person is not dealt with, the potential for racial violence always remains. To assert that you can believe whatever you want as long as no one is hurt is likely to lead to someone being hurt. Relativism fails to deal with the inner demons that drive us because of its general assertion that we create our own personal truth. To deal with the garbage that we often create, we need a standard of truth that does not waver and that can hold us accountable for hateful thoughts.

A second problem with the relativistic stance is that once relativism leaves the realm of personal philosophy or truth, it must control either none or all of our actions. Most, if not all, of our actions affect other humans. The relativist may argue, for example, that sexual relations outside of marriage are not wrong as long as they are between two consenting adults. But is this still true in the age of AIDS and failing marriages? Even if the adults are not married to others and do not have AIDS, does not the ease with which they enter into sexual relations contribute to a general promiscuous attitude within this nation? Does not such an attitude contribute to the very problems of AIDS, teenage pregnancy, and broken marriages? If pregnancy occurs, decisions must be made that will affect the well-being of another life. What started out as a decision between consenting adults now has ramifications that touch other lives.

If relativism regulates any action that affects others, then it must regulate all actions, since just about every action affects others. The only solution, then, for the relativist is to regulate none of our actions. Thus we are back to square one where to make morality relative is to make any individual action, including racist actions, acceptable.

From a relativistic viewpoint we could not have told South Africa that apartheid was wrong. It was the system that their society had chosen. Economically, blacks under that system did not seem to be any worse off than other blacks in Africa. We cannot tell the Klan that its attitude is wrong. They have a right to look after the interests of their own people. Is this not rational? We cannot condemn racial violence in many neighborhoods today. Is not the protection of one's neighborhood an admirable goal? Is it not rational to stay with one's own kind? What about the actions of violent minority street gangs? Their violence is a natural response to the racism they have had to endure throughout their lives. Ethical relativism suggests a rationality that cannot criticize this type of solution to problems. Because it refuses to recognize any moral absolutes, this system of morality fails to allow us the opportunity to bring true justice and harmony to our culture.

Holy Absolutes

Our belief in God is a necessary component of combating racism. After all, if we don't believe in God, what does it really matter if a bunch of white cosmic accidents are abusing a bunch of black cosmic accidents? There is absolutely no significance in protesting such a situation. If humans truly have no real worth, then one can justify using others as tools or chattel to achieve one's own goals. True justice needs the holy absolutes that are available to us through our Christian faith.

I can now say that racism is wrong! To the South African who claims that it is not wrong to oppress his black neighbors as long as they enjoy a minimum living standard, I say racism is wrong. God did not send his Son to die for someone who is less than human. You do not have the right to treat anyone as less than human.

To the black man who seethes with hatred for whites and constantly looks for ways to express that hatred, I say racism is wrong. Yes, we have been oppressed throughout history, but hatred does not justify hatred. Our Lord dealt with hatred by giving love. Those you hate, even those who deserve your hate, were also created by a loving Lord. Fight racial injustice but do not succumb to hatred or you will become like the one you have hated.

113

To the young tough who feels that he must defend his turf against an unwelcome intrusion of minorities, I say racism is wrong. You may be acting on some legitimate social problems, but the solution to those problems does not lie in your fist. The solution lies in your heart. God desires that all of us learn to live in harmony with one another.

The humanist, who does not believe in God, can do many fine works, but those works must come strictly out of the goodness of his or her heart. The humanist has no external standard on which to base a belief in racial justice. Thus whether an individual with a humanistic mindset chooses to help or hurt individuals of other races is an arbitrary, rational decision. However, when we are faithful to our religion and to our beliefs as Christians, we have consistent philosophical support in our fight against racism.

23

It Takes Two

> The price of hating other human beings is loving oneself less.
> Eldridge Cleaver
> *Soul on Ice*

It is so easy for a minority to become discouraged in this nation. The structure of American society is under the control of white Americans, and institutional racism cannot end until those who have the power decide to end it. As long as whites choose to defend their privileged places, minority groups will be denied opportunities in America. Minorities often feel that they are totally powerless to make significant progress in the ending of racism until whites become as aware of the need to end racism as minorities are.

This is also true in the church. It is white churches that have power and control because they have the greater access to the most powerful members of our society. It seems likely that racism within the church will continue until the members of the white church in America begin to realize the extent of the problem and are willing to apply themselves to creating solutions to this problem. If we are hoping that the church will take the lead in eradicating racism in our society, it is essential that white churches be committed to that goal.

However, minorities must not sell themselves short. We are important in the fight against racism. Indeed a healthy relationship between blacks and whites will not be possible until blacks are willing to work at that relationship as well as whites. Structural racism is something that whites do to blacks, but blacks can be just as guilty of personal racism as any white individual. This is sin no matter what race one may be.

The Proper Response

What is to be the proper response of black Christians to the evil of racism? Truly there is the temptation to allow the atrocities of the past to build into a hatred and bitterness toward whites. It would not be hard to construct a solid case against whites so that I can feel justified in putting them down. I can find plenty of reasons to distrust whites if I choose to do so. Yet this path leads me to a rejection of whites, which means I must accept and trust only blacks. Then I am not working in the interests of the human race but of the black race. I am no better than a black Klansman. This approach will only add to the current level of hostility between the races. A truly Christian response will rise above the natural worldly response that would lead us into a battle of racial special interest groups.

We have seen an application of this special-interest-group philosophy in the sort of "black power" that says the answer to the racial tension of this nation is in making sure African Americans have sufficient political power. It is assumed that only when blacks have the power to counter the evil of whites will equality come. I have to reject this approach, not because blacks do not deserve more power in this society. We do. To advocate taking power away from whites in a forceful, even if legal, manner places an emphasis on strife with which I am uncomfortable. If we choose to justify our place in society by power, then we can have our place in society taken away by that same power. Therefore white backlash becomes justified because whites have just as much right to take by power as we have to gain by power. It should not be power that affords blacks a say in the functioning of society, but rather the human right for African Americans to have a fair share of societal control.

When King's nonviolent leadership was no longer available to the Civil Rights movement, and more radical leaders took over, the movement seemed to lose some of its authority in this nation. We stopped making gains on the basis of a just cause and started making gains due to the power that we had accumulated. The result has been that, in the eyes of many Americans, the Civil Rights movement has been reduced to just another special-interest group. We are no longer seen as a movement with a moral high ground, but one that just wants our share of the pie.

A lasting solution to racism in our society must involve both minority and majority members in such a way that everyone can participate in the healing of the races. If we minorities continue to try to force a solution through power, I fear that we will eventually shut our white brothers and sisters out of this process, no matter how sympathetic they may become to our needs. In doing so we will forever segment our society into racial categories.

I'm not advocating that minorities give up the power we've gained. For example, it would be foolish to abandon our ability to create just laws through political pressure. But we must realize that power and love often work counter to each other. As a Christian I am called to love my white brothers and sisters, even before I am called to protect my own rights. I must be as eager to serve them as I am to serve individuals of my own race. Thus the challenge is to figure out how to wisely use any power that I have. It must never be merely for my own sake, but I must also have the welfare of others in mind. I believe that if minority leaders based their decisions about how to deal with racism on such a criterion, we might see more real change and less penny-ante politics.

Heart Change

The more I think about my responsibility as a Christian, the more I conclude that I must seek out ways to make more than just superficial changes in this culture. Changing laws, while important, is only a superficial way of dealing with racism. Racism will end only when changes happen at the heart level. Thus as a Christian I am committed to seeking out ways to produce this sort of heart change that is so desperately needed.

Some may complain that since minorities are the ones who have faced oppression, they should not have to be concerned about the hearts of those who may continue to oppress us. This is an understandable sentiment and a natural one, but it leads to a trap of hate. As Christians we must love those who may continue to hate us. Only then can we escape from feeling that our anger is justified and that we are free to reduce whites to a stereotype that we can easily hate. We must not give back to whites what we and our ancestors have received from them throughout history. Our concern for white individuals may help bring them out of their prison of hatred, even as we escape building our own prison.

It seems to me that often the minorities who are the most angry at whites are also the ones who seem to take the least personal responsibility for their own shortcomings. They seem to want to blame their failures on whites

117

instead of recognizing the possibility that they may have personally played a role in deciding their fate. It is not clear to me whether this same phenomenon is true for hateful whites, but I suspect that it might be. What is clear is that anger can become a shield behind which we hide to escape taking responsibility. We are not able to deal with the sins in our own lives because we are too busy hating the sins in the lives of others.

It is not that anger is never the appropriate response, but the Christian must be careful in his or her use of anger. At times anger is proper. The Bible states that we are not to sin in our anger (Eph. 4:26). So there is a proper time for anger. I believe that it's appropriate to be angry about the evil and the uselessness of racism. When we see any individual discriminated against then anger is proper. Whenever someone is devalued on the basis of a physical characteristic that he or she has no control over then anger is appropriate. It is right. It is right because abusing another person through racism is mocking the Lord who created that person. To treat someone as defective goods because of skin color is implying that sometimes God makes junk. That should cause every Christian of every color to be angry.

I must be careful not to sin in my anger, even if it is proper anger. For example, if I am insulted because of my race, it is proper that I should feel anger. No one should devalue me in that way, not because of how good I personally am, but because of the Lord who made me. Out of my anger I may confront that person in a loving manner so that he may become aware of his sin. If I allow that anger to linger, however; if I talk about that person behind his back rather than lovingly confronting him with his sin; if I hate him and hold a grudge against him, then my anger has not been manifested in a righteous way. Rather than being used to tear down the walls between us, it has become a tool of division that makes the situation worse. Any anger, even justified anger, can be carried to an extent to where it becomes sin. Wisely did the Lord command us not to allow the sun to go down on our anger.

What must be the response of minority Christians to racism? It must be love. It must be forgiveness. I am not talking about the sort of weak forgiveness that ignores the sins of the past. Ignoring an individual's sin is not necessarily showing love to that person. We may have to confront our white brothers and sisters about the sin of racism in their lives and in the society around them. This must be done in love, not out of a power trip or for personal gain. When we lovingly confront our white brothers and sisters, we gain the ability to take an important first step toward the sort of honest reconciliation that I believe God wants us to achieve.

Minority Christians are not powerless in this process of reconciliation. We do not have to merely wait for white Christians to become enlightened about the problems of racism. We can further the process along by loving our brothers and sisters and opening up the dialogue that must take place between the races. We can find the strength needed to love them and to forgive them when necessary. We can also look to them for love and forgiveness as the relationship between us grows stronger. It is going to take two, the minority and the majority, to rescue us from the racial mess that we have made. We must not allow ourselves to believe lies that say we are helpless to do anything about this situation or that we need more power to effect change. Instead we must get to the business of building the body of Christ into all that it was meant to be.

Beyond Black and White

You shall love your neighbor as yourself.
Matthew 22:39

It sometimes is amazing what the Lord can use to teach us. For example, I was able to learn something from the O. J. Simpson trial. I got so tired of the trial. It had all the elements of sensationalism: a celebrity, murder, and sex. But as we focused on this one spectacle, the battle over health care was raging, massacres were breaking out in Africa, and Congress was preparing for mid-term elections. The abnormal, or even sick, interest in the trial while all of these vital events were happening around us only confirmed my fear that we have lost our marbles.

Poll after poll has revealed that Americans differ along racial lines as to whether Simpson is guilty of the crime. Blacks are more likely to believe that Simpson is innocent than whites. Essentially we had a murder case where all the evidence was played out before the public. Both black and white Americans had access to the same evidence. Yet the races have different perceptions about this evidence. Why should this be the case?

One may argue that the reaction to the Simpson trial is symbolic of individual racial perceptions in this nation. African Americans may be able to relate to Simpson in ways that whites cannot. Our history has made us suspicious of our judicial system, and it's easy to think that Simpson may have been exploited by it. African Americans have good reason to be wary of our criminal justice system. Studies have shown that blacks are likely to serve longer jail sentences for similar crimes than are whites, police deal more harshly with blacks than with whites, and a black youth is likely to be charged with a more severe crime for the same act as committed by a white youth.[1] Furthermore, individuals who murder whites are more likely to wind up on death row than individuals who murder blacks.[2] If Simpson had been found guilty, it may have represented yet another black victim of an unfair system.

Naturally most white Americans do not see the O. J. case in this way. I am not quick to attribute racial factors to their response, but the fact that the accused is black and the victims are white probably plays a role in their belief about Simpson's guilt or innocence. But probably even more important is the fact that whites are able to divorce themselves from the racial implications that are at hand and treat this case like any other murder trial. They do not perceive the racial implications, because for most of them those implications do not mean very much. Since they cannot relate to being part of a group that has historically suffered in the criminal justice system, they fail to understand why African Americans are making such a big deal about this.

I have found that this lack of awareness is not unusual among white Americans. Many of my white friends have confessed to me that they have never considered racial issues before in their life. This is to be expected since it is very possible for white Americans to go through life never having to deal with racial prejudice or discrimination in any meaningful way. They don't have to deal with these issues unless they choose to do so.

Racial minorities, however, must not only often confront the hatred and bias of whites, but they must often contend with situations where those who put them down also have power over them. Thus, in America, all racial minorities come to some point in their lives where they deal with the issue of race. They may choose to ignore it or deny it, but even these responses are ways of dealing with it.

These different life experiences help to explain why there are differences in the way the races perceive the Simpson case and differences in the way they see life in general. I am forced to consider as part of my identity the fact that I am a black man. Therefore, to some extent, I must take into account those who are similar to me—other blacks—when I form my perception of reality. Since we share similar social interests, our view of society will be highly correlated. I am forced to think about the interest of that group when I think about reality. Now this is not to say that all of my thoughts are determined by those group interests but the fact that I have to take such interests into account at all is troubling. I am forced to see the world in black and white.

Everyone in America sees the world in black and white to some extent. The issue that best reveals this tendency is affirmative action.

The main reason this issue divides us is that each group thinks about this issue in terms of its own interests. Most blacks are for affirmative action because it works to our advantage. So we defend our support with terms such as "historical justice" and "institutional discrimination." Most whites oppose it because affirmative action works against them. They defend their opposition with terms such as "reverse discrimination" and "meritocracy." All the while, both groups, if they were to be honest, would tell you that it is in their group's interest to take such a position. Individuals may, at least indirectly, gain from their particular beliefs concerning affirmative action, and so their beliefs are at least partially selfish in nature.

This is what racism has reduced us to: groups that struggle against each other for the goods that this society has to offer. The replacement of individual selfishness with group selfishness is not a step toward Christian morality—not exactly what the Bible paints as the proper image of the church. The solution is to break out of this tendency to see in black and white. We must somehow find a way to see past our own group's interest and find solutions to the racial issues that surround us.

As far as affirmative action is concerned, minorities are correct when they point out that the historical conditions of this nation have set into motion processes that now work against them. Affirmative action is one way to restore fairness in a society that has traditionally been unfair to some of its members. Whites are correct, however, when they assert that some of these programs sometimes discriminate unfairly against them and that merit should be the factor by which they are judged. Affirmative action programs that are out of control can tend to produce some of the same inequities that Jim Crow laws used to produce.

Who is right? Perhaps a solution can be found if we look beyond the specter of group and personal interests that fuel these arguments. Let me offer a possible third perspective.

Historical discrimination is a problem that has built racism into our very institutions. Affirmative action or some variety of it is necessary to correct these wrongs. Like many government programs, however, affirmative action can take on a life of its own and no longer serve in the interest of justice. It may only serve to give minority groups the ability to exploit the majority group. A time comes when this type of program must be put to an end. Though necessary at one time in our history, it can build new types of racial bias in a system that we eventually want to become color-blind. If we never rid ourselves of programs such as affirmative action, we are subtly stating that racial minorities can never fully compete on a par with whites and will always need help. I think that no racial minority wants to accept such a premise.

Even if my assessment of affirmative action programs is correct, I have not solved anything in a political sense. Is this the right time for the programs to end or do they need to go on longer? That is a subjective judgment that once again falls prey to group self-interest. To deal with that question we must go beyond what our own group's interest may be and look to the interest of those who are not in our group. We cannot look just at how a particular program may benefit us, but we must ask whether fairness and justice will continue to be served by such programs. This is as radical as Jesus' concept of turning the other cheek. But this philosophy is not completely foreign to modern society. Martin Luther King Jr. was pursuing fairness and justice for all of society when he advocated nonviolence to end racial discrimination. It was his desire to save whites from their own hatred as well as to end injustice for blacks. The answer to affirmative action, or any racial issue, can be found only when we die to self, to our racial identity, and to our desire to better the fortunes of our race, and indirectly our own fortunes. Unless we honestly deal with the biases that benefit us, we will always be able to rationalize pushing the issues that happen to serve our own best interests. Only as we turn to Christ can we ever hope to be truly selfless and motivated to devise fair ways to meet the competing needs of both minorities and whites.

Part of the fallen nature of humans is that we too often fail to take our own failures into account while we amplify the failures of those who are different from us. In this way we can justify having more power and authority than those who are different. It is natural for us to attempt to ignore our sin nature. It is often not a pretty sight, but as Christians we have the opportunity to acknowledge that nature so that we can combat the ills of this society. The illness of racism can never be fully dealt with until we Christians lead the way, willing to look at our own depravity before finding fault with other groups.

When we begin to move away from our own group's interests and take into account the interests of others who are of a different race or ethnicity, then we begin to develop the mindset that is necessary for reconciliation to take place. Only with this mindset will we be able to make decisions that foster good relationships with others, rather than decisions that merely protect our place in society. Through Christ it is possible for me to reject societal norms that attach importance to race. Instead of seeing black, white, Asian, or Native American I can begin to see the human race. Death to one's own interest can be liberating as it opens one up to the ability to develop a love for others that can bring an end to our racial hatreds and fears.

We can rise above black and white in this nation by adopting a vision that encompasses all races. As Christians we have access to a philosophy that will allow us to do just that. The fact that we still see things from a black or white perspective, instead of just from a human perspective, speaks as much to the failure of the church to become the unifying light our society needs as to the natural selfish tendency of humans.

Forgive Us This Day

The line separating good and evil passes not through states, nor between classes, nor between parties either—but right through every human heart.

Alexander Solzhenitsyn
The Gulag Archipelago 1918–1956

The Need for Repentance

Perhaps the most central concept of the Christian faith is the concept of repentance. We repent when we recognize our sinfulness. It is in repentance that we realize how much we need external help. Repentance helps us see that we are unable to make it on our own. One can argue that if a person does not have an accurate perception of repentance, he may not have a real relationship with the Lord.

The way repentance is expressed in Christianity differs from all other world religions. Other world religions may recognize the fact that we have fallen short of the mark that the deity wants for us; however, we are encouraged to keep trying. We may eventually reach the mark. So one strives for the five pillars of the faith in Islam or the eightfold path in Buddhism. The Christian concept of sin means that we have messed up and will continue to mess up. As Christians we do not believe that we are sinners because we sin but that we sin because we are sinners. Being sinners then is who we are all the time, not just now and then.

Once we recognize that fact, it is easy to see that we humans are truly depraved. Without Christ we would be doomed to hell, as well as doomed to live out our lives in this state of depravity. Even with Christ we recognize that in this life we will never be perfect. Every now and then we may backslide or fall prey to that sin nature. With Christ and through the new nature he gives us, we can gain the strength to honestly deal with the sins in our lives and to develop the character that the Lord wants us to have.

The process of repentance can only begin when we are willing to recognize the sin in our lives. God cannot deal with a sin that we are not willing to admit that we have. A drug addict must admit that he or she has a problem before realizing the need for help. Likewise God can help only those individuals who look to him for help. To allow the Lord to help us, we must begin the process of repentance by admitting our sin.

Easier said than done. I believe that the main reason why individuals who learn about the gospel do not become Christians is because of their unwillingness to repent. To do so means to admit that they are wrong and that the way they have chosen to live their lives is corrupt. No one likes to recognize this fact. Our natural tendency is to set a standard we know we can achieve. Then we use that standard to prove to ourselves that we are good people. Everyone, no matter how evil he or she may be, likes to think he or she is good. Rapists may comfort themselves with the fact that they are not murderers. And vice versa. Thieves justify their crimes by their socioeconomic status. Some Christians are sexually promiscuous but are proud that they don't sleep with married individuals.

Repentance crushes these false standards by forcing us to admit that there is an external standard that we cannot reach. Thus we must look to our Lord for help.

Repenting of Racism

What does all of this have to do with racism? Plenty. Racism is sin and where there is racism there is a need for repentance. Our growth as Christians depends on our willingness to concede that we need the Lord to help us deal with our sin. He would have us repent of all sin, including racism. That is the only effective way of dealing with it.

This is where Christ can save us. Because he forgives us of our sinfulness, we have in him the security to admit it to ourselves. This sort of honesty is vital to the growth of every healthy Christian. It obviously is applicable to more than the racial issue. No Christian will be able to enjoy all that the Christian life has to offer until he or she is able to honestly admit his or her failings and then know the reassurance of the Savior's love and grace. This is the great advantage that Christians enjoy over adherents to every other world religion. Christianity deals directly with sin in such a way that we do not have to perform to receive God's acceptance. He gives us the confidence to dare to live as a holy Lord would want us to live.

Beyond the importance it has for our personal growth, confronting our sin nature is vital if there is going to be a solution to the racial issue. Individuals of all races must be willing to confront the sin nature that is within them. We all must face issues of guilt, anger, and bitterness. We must find ways to be honest with each other, to have an open communication so that we can understand each other and build a new relationship between the races.

In accepting the forgiveness that Christ has offered us, we can be free from the need to justify our sins of racism. We can admit the negative feelings that we may have toward members of other races and be free to develop an open and honest relationship with them. We Christians must take the lead in forging the type of genuine reconciliation that we need, because we know the way. It is the only way to get beyond the hatred that we have allowed to fester for so long.

Repentance can be painful, and we often search for ways to escape it. People will deny that they are racists to avoid repentance. Statements like "I have a good friend who is black" or "I will hire a Hispanic who is qualified" often are used to mask the racism that lies within a person's heart. The path to racial healing must begin with a painful and honest assessment of the manifestations of racism in our lives.

An interesting aspect of race relations is the way we so clearly see the sin of others while ignoring our own sin. Racial minorities are sensitive to white racism yet are ignorant of their own bitterness. Whites often accurately perceive the vindictiveness of racial minorities yet do not see their own insensitivity to the problems that minorities face. The problem is that we seek out the speck in our brother's or sister's eye while forgetting about the log in our own eye. In this respect racism does not differ from any other sin.

The problem is that this is not the biblical way of handling sin. The biblical model of dealing with sin is for us to examine ourselves first, allow our Lord to purify us, and then encourage others to deal with their sins. We point to sins in others only after we have repented of our own sins. Our own process of repentance allows us to help others out of love and without condemnation. Only by approaching others in an attitude of repentance can we begin an honest process where individuals from different races can work to heal each other of the sickness of racism.

Corporate Repentance

Part of that honest dealing with sin can lead us to what might seem like strange verses in the Bible. In Nehemiah 1:6–7 we read:

> Let Thine ear now be attentive and Thine eyes open to hear the prayer of Thy servant which I am praying before Thee now, day and night, on behalf of the sons of Israel Thy servants, confessing the sins of the sons of Israel which we have sinned against Thee; I and my father's house have sinned. We have acted very corruptly against Thee and have not kept the commandments, nor the statutes, nor the ordinances which Thou didst command Thy servant Moses.

And again in Daniel 9:5–6:

> We have sinned, committed iniquity, acted wickedly, and rebelled, even turning aside from Thy commandments and ordinances. Moreover, we have not listened to Thy servants the prophets, who spoke in Thy name to our kings, our princes, our fathers, and all the people of the land.

In each case the writer repents, not for his own personal sin but for the sin of his nation. This is hard for us Americans to understand because we have such an individualistic culture. But if these passages are examples for us to follow, obviously the Lord wants us to deal with the sins of our nation as well. Why would this be?

Perhaps it is because the Lord knows that sins from the past often continue to impact the present until the process of repentance is begun. Both Daniel and Nehemiah knew that Israel was suffering because of past sins. These particular passages deal with sins that they had not personally committed but that were having devastating consequences nonetheless and undoubtedly contributing to the current sins of Israel. Today, in this society, we are suffering the consequences of sins that were committed in the past.

Whites are often dismayed when racial minorities attribute characteristics such as bigotry to them. Their response is often: "That was the sin of my father but it is not my sin." But the effects of this sin cannot

128

be denied, nor can the fact that whites benefit today from the historic advantage claimed by their ancestors. Whether it is laws of seniority that work against minorities who cannot have held jobs as long as whites, standards for assessing credit risk that work against minorities who lack the conventional credit references, or admission rules that favor the descendants of alumni in prestigious colleges that were until recently all white, these rules discriminate against minorities because of the historic advantage that whites have enjoyed in this country. Such rules are woven into the structure of society and are simply taken for granted. Whites would not question their validity if minorities had not begun to challenge them. Now it is incumbent on whites to recognize the impact of the sin of their ancestors and repent of it.

Personal repentance is not adequate. There must also be corporate repentance if we are to honestly deal with racism. It can be tempting for whites to believe that they are not guilty of the sin of racism because they have not personally committed acts of bigotry. But this distorts the fact that today's majority group members have benefited from their ancestors' acts against minorities.

We struggle against this type of repentance. Repentance of our own personal sins is hard enough. Now God is calling us to repent of sins committed by our ancestors. But just as Daniel and Nehemiah were willing to repent on behalf of the nation to rescue Israel from oppression, we can seek this type of repentance to save our nation from the enslavement of racism. This type of repentance must begin in the church and then spread to the rest of society. I have hope that this may be happening. The recent public repentance of the sin of racism on the part of the Southern Baptist Convention is encouraging. I hope that this may be part of a growing trend.

When this sort of repentance takes place, then we are presented with the wonderful possibility of reconciliation. True reconciliation is only possible on a spiritual plane. It is impossible as merely a legal reality. Like an estranged couple, the races have been separated through sin and continual misunderstandings. Whites have set up mechanisms that help hide their historic sins, and racial minorities are choked by bitterness. Racial tensions and mistrust keep mounting and both groups sin against each other.

God's promise is that repentance can bring restoration. It is possible for the races to have true fellowship with each other. The hope is that one day we may drop the prejudices that have kept us apart and enjoy what each other has to offer. This is like the reconciliation that lovers must go through to save a relationship. Painful issues must be dealt with, wrongs must be forgiven and forgotten, and the qualities of each other must be appreciated.

Reconciliation then is the goal of repentance. However, the Lord is going to force us to work through important issues in order to obtain this goal. We are going to have to intentionally seek reconciliation through repentance. The task of the church is to intentionally create an atmosphere of acceptance in which we can enter into relationships where we are comfortable enough to be honest about past and present sins. This can begin the process of racial healing. To do anything less is to turn our back on the problem of racism and to leave that problem to a secular society that does not have the spiritual equipment to deal with this sin.

Talk Shows, Jobs, and Interracial Dating

> You blind guides, who strain out a gnat and swallow a camel! Woe to you, scribes and Pharisees, hypocrites! For you clean the outside of the cup and of the dish, but inside they are full of robbery and self-indulgence.
>
> Matthew 23:24–25

Because I study interracial relationships, I used to watch daytime talk shows when that topic was being discussed. The academic content of such shows is usually pretty poor; however, I find that they are useful in revealing much about the common attitude of the public toward interracial relationships, especially interracial marriage. One should understand that in order to boost their ratings the producers of these shows go out of their way to find the most outrageous people to interview. So when they deal with interracial relationships, the guests inevitably include relatives who have disowned the interracial couple for breaking the taboo against such marriages.

Usually the audience will ask these disgruntled family members whether or not they are racist. Usually they say no, and yet they have berated and disowned a family member who is dating or has married someone of another race. Now if the simple definition of a racist is someone who treats other individuals differently based on race, these family members *are* racist. How can they deny their racist actions and attitudes?

In the abstract, racism is perceived as a social evil and most people don't want to be associated with evil. The very nature of sin is that we want to engage in it, since it is usually pleasurable, without having our activity defined as sin. Likewise individuals who find it easy to engage in racist activity do not want such activity to be defined as racist.

As we have already seen, this is a common component of sin. We don't want our sin defined as sin, so we set standards we know we can achieve. In this respect these racists are no different than any of us. They define racism in such a way that their actions are not racist. Then they don't have to take responsibility for their own personal racism. Here is another example:

> A small-time collector for the Syndicate casually refers to "shines," "spades," "jigs," "loads of coal." When asked whether he considers himself a racist, he is indignant: . . . no! Did you hear me say "nigger"? Never![1]

Each of us has sin we must confront. None of us has the right to feel superior to anyone else. We have an obligation to confront others with their sin and we need others to confront us with our sin. It is important that we see racism as sin and not as a personal preference. Any rejection of an interracial relationship on the basis of race alone is racism.

There usually are special circumstances that cause individuals to reject interracial relationships and be unwilling to acknowledge their racism. Interracial marriages may threaten people in ways that they are not always willing to admit. Perhaps this can best be seen in work done in the 1940s by Gunnar Myrdal. According to his understanding of white ideology, whites desire to maintain dominance over blacks in certain areas more than in others. The priority of these areas of dominance is as follows:

1. First, and most importantly, to prevent intermarriage between blacks and whites.
2. Then maintenance of social hierarchy. This involves behaviors of dominance and submission surrounding handshaking, forms of address, and the like.
3. Then segregation of public facilities.
4. Then denial of the vote.
5. Then discrimination by police and courts.
6. Finally, and lastly, economic domination in jobs and such.[2]

This list seems to reveal that whites don't necessarily want blacks to suffer; they just want them to stay away. The typical well-meaning white in the '40s probably wanted African Americans to be fairly compensated for any work they did, but that same white probably would have been disturbed if a black moved next door to him or her. And heaven help that black person if he attempted to date a sibling or a daughter of that white individual. Racism is divided into two dimensions. One is more structural and economic: whether minorities can vote or hold jobs or be treated fairly by the police. The second dimension is a personal one: whether one will accept minorities in intimate and semi-intimate situations.

Today, a half century after Myrdal's analysis, we still see the two dimensions of racism. Some of the issues may have changed but the two dimensions remain the same. The white individuals on the talk shows are likely to accept minorities at their place of employment. Most would have no problem even working for an African American. Perhaps having one live in the neighborhood would be no big deal. This is because such relationships are economical and can be somewhat impersonal. These same individuals are having a hard time with their relatives' dating or marrying minorities because such relationships add a personal nature to their interaction with minorities. They are able to act in a nonracist manner as long as minorities "stay in their place."

The acceptance of different races in economic relations has become the standard for measuring racism in our society. If you have harmonious relationships with minorities at the economic level, you aren't racist. This, however, does not involve dealing with minorities on a personal level. As long as we allow such a redefinition of racism we will continue to mandate the separation of races because in this acceptable dimension of racism we do not have to try to understand each other on a personal level. Integration programs become meaningless as the different races refuse to relate on a level that is intimate enough to allow many of their fears and suspicions of other races to dissipate. Perhaps this is the reason why the acceptance of intermarriage is such a useful measure of the level of acceptance that the races have for each other.[3]

Structural and economic equality should never be enough for us as Christians. This may be the place for the laws—and we should press for such laws—but structural change will never be enough by itself to erase the attitudes of racial superiority. Personal racism, however, can be confronted only in institutions that deal honestly with sin. These should be our churches.

Our churches, however, have not often dealt with the issue of racism nor helped their members understand that racism can have a personal component to it as well as an economic one. Christians have not developed an adequate answer to the question of interracial relationships due to our general neglect of racial issues. Therefore many Christians have a difficult time accepting interracial romantic relationships. This reveals a problem with personal racism.

When we allow fellow brothers or sisters in Christ to hide behind their acceptance of economic integration to cover up their aversion to interracial romantic relationships, we are not doing them a favor. Anytime we allow an individual's sin to go unchallenged, we are being less than faithful friends. Through loving relationships we can help build the bridges between the races that not only bring economic and legal fairness to members of the minority races, but also can bring the sort of interracial relationships that may help to correct some of the distorted ideas that racism in our society has given us.

When the church refuses to deal with the personal components of racism, it begins to give up its moral legitimacy. The message the church gives to racial minorities is that the church is not a place for healing but an institution that is satisfied with the status quo, even when that status quo is unjust. It's risky to confront individuals who hide behind an acceptance of economic equality but do not want to deal with personal relationships between the races. It may drive some of these individuals out of our fellowship. Some may hold powerful positions in the church, making such confrontations even more difficult. But is it right to ignore one sin but confront other sins? Would we not confront a deacon who is having an adulterous affair? When the church becomes as serious about racism as it is about sexual sin, many of the barriers of hypocrisy, which separate the races and water down our witness to society, will be torn down.

If the church is going to be serious about dealing with racism, we must be willing to confront structural racism. More than that, the church must provide an environment that encourages the sort of personal relationships that will allow us to deal with our own individual fears that often prevent us from accepting each other. This is not to say that the church must attempt to pressure its members into entering into romantic interracial relationships. As I stated before, that would only encourage poor relationships, based on political correctness rather than godly

134

principles. The decision to date interracially is one that every individual Christian must make. But we must have an atmosphere that is accepting of such relationships as well as close and intimate nonromantic relationships between the races. It seems likely that it is when we begin to understand each other in close friendships that we will develop the empathy and love that Christ wants us to have for all of our Christian family members.

27

One in Christ

There is neither Jew nor Greek, there is neither slave nor free man,
there is neither male nor female; for you are all one in Christ Jesus.

Galatians 3:28

It can be an interesting experience to read a list of student organizations on our college campuses. The list of Christian organizations often goes something like this: Black Christian Fellowship, Chinese Bible Study, Korean Bible Study, Latino Christian Students. Before whites get too comfortable, I should remind them that the Christian organizations that they are a part of—InterVarsity Christian Fellowship and Campus Crusade for Christ—have become synonymous with "White Christian Ministry."

As a sociologist I am forced to ask why a group of individuals who profess the same general beliefs chooses to divide itself along racial lines? The first place to look for an answer is at that belief system itself. Does Christianity employ a cognitive system that supports this form of separatism? Even a cursory reading of the Gospels or Paul's letters reveals that this type of separatism is not part of Christian theology. Whatever is causing Christians to separate themselves racially is not due to any message that we receive from our doctrines.

A better explanation of why Christians seem so intent on separating themselves along racial lines may be that we live in a society that encourages our separation. The Christian community has chosen to endorse the values of our society rather than living out the values that Christ called us to. We ignore the commandment to love and we shrug off our responsibility to begin to create God's kingdom here on earth.

We live in a racist society, and it is clear that the church has been called to bring about reconciliation, to heal the wounds that racism has caused.

136

Separation into different racial groups for fellowship and worship will not bring about reconciliation. In fact it can only add to the problem. We can live out what we say we believe about equality and tolerance by coming together as Christians of different races within the same fellowship. This can begin the healing process.

Ultimately one cannot separate moral beliefs from the moral actions that support those beliefs. However, research has shown that often our specific actions fail to be consistent with our stated beliefs. For example, surveys from the 1960s show that while about 60 percent of the people believed that individuals had a right to live where they wanted to live, only 38 percent of them would be willing to have a black family live near them.[1] There is obviously an inconsistency between the beliefs and actions of the respondents, which leads one to think that what individuals say they believe and what they actually believe are not the same thing. When the beliefs of people are inconsistent with their actions, those people are not being intellectually honest. Christians must ensure that they never fall into such a trap. A racist worldview is incompatible with a Christian worldview. Our beliefs and actions must be consistent; therefore we must show the world what a Christian worldview is by working to eradicate the racism, no matter how subtle, that we find within our churches. I think that one can make the case that the way we have separated ourselves racially in our different fellowships reveals how racism has affected the church. It is imperative that Christians begin to take actions that will reverse this trend.

We must be realistic. The actions that will be necessary will not be easy to take. They will come at a cost. Some of us will have to go into uncomfortable situations to integrate our churches. I know that I would be quite uncomfortable going to a Korean Bible study. They may be uncomfortable accepting me into their group. But this kind of step is what is necessary if we are serious about developing Christian ministries that are truly inclusive.

What am I calling for? To be honest I am calling the church to a deliberate action that will challenge the racial barriers that we have placed about us. Even something as simple as going to the Bible study of a different ethnic group may prove to be very meaningful. In fact such actions may be indispensable if we are to deal with segregation in our pews. The natural course of our tendency to separate may never be broken unless some of us begin to take deliberate action that challenges the way we choose to separate ourselves. American history has proven that racial barriers have tremendous staying power. Tearing down those barriers will take concerted effort. We as Christians must become part of the solution; otherwise, we are probably part of the problem.

Please do not misunderstand. I believe that there is a time for separation on the basis of cultural similarity. Individuals from a certain culture must spend time within that culture discovering what they are all about. Then they know what they have to offer the rest of society. I would not want to eliminate any Christian fellowship that has a strong racial or ethnic component. But while it may be important to keep some contact with one's own racial group it is important not to forget the real goal of the church. That goal is to represent the body of Christ in all of its wonderful diversity. To escape into a racial enclave is useful only if it allows that group of individuals to prepare to give of itself to the entire Christian body. Therefore I believe that even while belonging to a group of one's ethnic peers, it is important to maintain membership in some integrated ministry that allows the individual to remember that true Christian fellowship must always be heading toward an inclusive culture.

We often assume that individuals of different races could not be interested in worshiping with us. We must put to death this idea. Some individuals may indeed be uncomfortable and turn down invitations. Others may come, become uncomfortable, and leave. But others will love it. They will see that it is a group of Christians—not blacks, whites, Asians, Hispanics, or whatever. This will begin to build the unity that the church so badly needs. We will see that despite some differences we all have one important similarity: We love the Lord. This one similarity is all we need to make us one.

28

Living in Sin

> Let us not sleep as others do, but let us be alert and sober.
> 1 Thessalonians 5:6

I think that we are often confused about what true morality is. We tend to equate it with sexual purity and not rebelling against certain rules and regulations. I think that we should redefine the term "living in sin" to have more than just a sexual reference. Living in sin is rebellion against the order that God established for us to live in. This rebellion may manifest itself sexually but often for evangelicals it manifests itself in attitudes that do not challenge the status quo when it should be challenged. If you live your life in such a way as to disrupt the process of racial justice or ignore the racial injustice that you see around you and pretend that harmony abounds, this is living in sin.

This seems like a radical definition of sin only because we have traditionally defined sin so that it is actually easy for us to attain righteousness, even without the help of our Lord. We construct a set of rules that reflect our society and then follow them. Then we can take pleasure in how righteous we are. Morality must be more than just abstaining from sexual activity and obeying the proper authorities. It consists of displaying the qualities of love and justice that our Lord showed. Quite simply, we are called to be as perfect as Christ (Matt. 5:48). But you see, none of us will ever obtain that goal in our lives. At the center of Christianity, and one of the things that distinguish it from any of the other world religions, is the fact that we can never make it on our own. Growth to the Christian consists of constantly trusting our Lord to help us in those areas we cannot handle by ourselves, while giving up control over aspects of our lives that we want to control. Whenever we fail to trust the Lord in such areas, whether it be sex, honesty, or race relations, then we are in rebellion and that rebellion is at the heart of all sin.

As Christians we are called to be salt in this society. That means that we do not deal only with the sin in ourselves but we are called to deal with the sin in society. In America that means taking an active stand against racial injustice as well as against promiscuity and pornography. Pornography and bigotry are equally ugly and abhorrent to our Lord.

We like to believe that we are a civilized and advanced society but we still cling to primitive rivalries and hatreds. We like to believe that discrimination and bigotry are a thing of the past but this belief only enables those sins to continue. Robert Merton coined the term *timid bigot.* It refers to individuals who harbor feelings of prejudice but who are afraid to discriminate. This is different from what he called a *true bigot,* one who is not afraid to openly discriminate.[1] Evidence of timid bigots can be seen in the success of politicians who play on racial hatreds.

In this society we have sinned. We have used false standards by which to judge others. We have known of injustice according to race and yet we have chosen to be silent about these injustices. We have failed to correct the cruelties of the past. It is not news to Christians that we live in a society in which sin abounds. However, Christians have been especially silent about dealing with the sin of racism. We have not challenged individuals who attempt to justify this sin through the Scriptures. Are we in our silence not as guilty as the blatant racist and bigot?

We have attempted to minister to those who hunger after racial righteousness and justice by giving them cotton candy, using methods that give temporary satisfaction but have no long-lasting effect. We try to satisfy them by saying, "I am not racist. Why, I have a friend who is black!" Or we state that we believe in racial equality, even though we dare not allow that to be preached from the pulpit. We claim to teach our children to be unprejudiced even though we are nervous if they develop friendships with individuals of different races of the opposite sex. In short, we lay claim to a general value of equality but we fail to live out that belief in the specific dimension of our lives.

Are we as Christians ever encouraged to marshal our energies to bring about racial justice? Are we encouraged to vote against a candidate who has shown disrespect for racial justice? George Kelsey states that Christians who are racist are really polytheistic.[2] Because of the inconsistencies of Christian and racist doctrines, those who attempt to hold to both use multiple meanings for assessing the worth of humans. On the one hand they state that all are equal but on the other hand they hold on to stereotypes that devalue individuals of other races. They are idolaters in that they attempt to find answers to the important metaphysical questions of meaning, using a source other than the Bible—their own racial beliefs. Perhaps one of the reasons that racism has had the ability to damage so many lives in the church is because we bring the idolatrous nature of racism directly into the church. We have allowed it to sit in the middle of our worship service and to entice our members without our even putting up a fuss. It is appropriate for the church to treat this idol as we would treat any other idol in the church: Cast it out in no uncertain terms.

When Jesus Christ came into our world, he came to bring reconciliation. He came to restore our relationship with our Father. We had rejected God's offer of love and companionship, rebelling and trying to find our own path. In Christ, the Creator of the universe came to be with us. He paid the price of the cross to correct the mistakes that we had made, to correct the lies we had chosen to live by. One of those lies is that we can evaluate people on the basis of the color of their skin. Because of our commonalty in Christ, we no longer have to base our worth on anything other than his love and we can be free to love others who do not look like us.

After Jesus' resurrection, he left his church here to continue the process of reconciling humans to God. This is the primary purpose of the church as far as its relationship to the world is concerned, but I do not believe that this is its only purpose in that relationship. Reconciliation was also meant to happen between humans. Just as our relationship to the Lord was severed in the fall, so too was our ability to truly love and accept others. Just as Jesus came to provide a means for rebuilding our relationship with our Lord, so too did he come to provide a means by which we can have true fellowship with others. This fellowship was never meant to be exclusive; rather, we are all to learn how to love and accept one another just as our Lord loves and accepts us. It is unfortunate that the church has not always lived up to its full responsibility in either of these tasks of reconciliation. However, sin in the past can never stop us from repentance in the present and obedience in the future.

Are we not in pain? Don't we cling to stereotypes of inferiority and mistrust? Has this not brought out feelings of hatred and bitterness? Yes,

141

we cover our pain quite well. We find a couple of members of different races to befriend so that we can tell ourselves that we are free of the disease of racism. Yet down deep inside we know that we are clinging to old patterns of mistrust. And because we never talk about this with our friends, we fail to see how widespread this disease is. It is then free to move on and invade other victims.

The body has suffered enough! Now is the time for healing. It is time for healing in the body and in society. The pain that we have denied can be eradicated and we can know the joy and the love of unconditional fellowship.

Reconciliation is possible. The church is full of individuals who lived a former life of total rebellion against the Lord. How many times have we heard testimonies of individuals who were involved in drugs, satanic worship, or depravity who turned their life over to the Lord and became totally new people? So too must we work to see individuals who are hardcore racists turn their lives over to Christ so that they can know the freedom that love can bring when it washes out the hatred that has lingered there for so long. We must work for the day when former embittered and resentful blacks worship with former hateful whites, both united in giving glory to the Lord.

I realize that I have not given in this book comprehensive answers to the problem of racism. Complete answers can only come after we have recognized the problem of racism and in repentance have entered into a dialogue with each other, seeking solutions. I have used this book to raise many issues and to start the process of dialogue that is necessary for us to begin to learn to love each other. I do not believe that the answers are as simple or as easy as we may like to think. The answers are going to be costly to individuals of all races as we shatter the myths that hide our responsibilities. True justice comes only to those who are willing to pay the radical price of self-denial.

The world that I would like to see, and I believe Christ would like to see, will be disturbing to some. I want to see a world where we treat each other as fully human and fully equal no matter what our race and nationality may be. It would be a world where the relationship I have with you is limited only by our personality differences, not our racial ones. Despite the lip service that many individuals have given to these goals, we in America are still a far cry from this type of society. I fear that there will be much more pain and suffering before we get to this new world. The question for those of us who call on Christ is whether we will be willing to endure the pain necessary to bring such a world about. Martin Luther King once talked about a dream where a person would never again be judged by the color of his skin. He talked of a dream where children of all colors would be able to walk hand in hand. This dream will not be realized by accident or as a natural course of events. Instead, Christians, relying on a magnificent God who can give us the strength that is necessary, can make this dream reality. This God can help us rise above our personal inadequacies so that we can over-turn centuries of historic mistrust and injustice. As Christians begin to deal with the difficult issues that surround racism, we will find new avenues of witness open to us, new opportunities of ministry, and new allies to work with us. My invitation to you is to join this process as our God gives us the grace to rebuild the bridges that we have allowed our sin to burn down.

PART 4

where do
WE GO
from
HERE?

Sometimes I wish that I had the gift of prophecy. It would be great if I could tell what God was doing and how it will affect the future. Where will I be in ten years? What will happen to my good friends? Who is going to win the Super Bowl? (I could make some money out of this!) The gift of prophecy would be of incredible importance when it comes to the issue of racism in our country. Maybe if I had that gift I could look into the future and tell you that everything is going to be just fine. By the year 2050, all the races in the United States are going to be living in harmony. Or maybe I will see a horrible race war that is going to devastate our nation. In that case all my struggling for reconciliation is in vain and I should just sit back and wait for the inevitable to happen. Maybe that is why the Lord does not allow us to see the future. Such a sight might easily inspire a fatalism that would cripple us.

So I don't have the gift of prophecy. That means that the future is not an open book to me and I must prepare to work as hard as I can to be a part of the healing process that our Lord desires. Unless you have the gift of prophecy I suggest that you do the same. Our future concerning race relations is up to us to set. We can look to the Lord and allow him to teach us racial harmony or we can look after our own interests and the interests of our racial group and continue down a path of mistrust and hatred.

At the end of a good Baptist sermon there is always an invitation. I guess this is my invitation. I want to touch not just your head but your heart as well. I hope to motivate God's people to take their rightful place in the struggle for the ending of racial barriers and encouraging racial reconciliation. If this book can somehow manage to do that, then the future may be bright after all.

Breaking the Cycles
of Hate

Train up a child in the way he should go,
Even when he is old he will not depart from it.
                                        Proverbs 22:6

There is evidence that children may learn to group together
by race by the age of three.[1] Think about that. They are segregating
themselves by the age of *three!* At that young age children have already
learned the messages of stratification that we have imbedded in our society. Because racism is not a natural phenomenon, we must be giving
racist messages to our children that they are picking up before their
fourth birthday. Therefore one can see that racism in our generation is
strongly ingrained into a cycle of hatred that is rapidly passed to the
next generation.

This can be a depressing thought. In spite of all of the legal and social
movements toward racial tolerance that we have seen in the past generation, children have begun to recognize by the age of three that we still
have a social expectation of racism. Perhaps their innocence and naive
nature reveal more about our current state of race relations than many of
us would like to admit. It is also depressing because part of the hope for
racial reconciliation lies in the children who are our future. If we can
teach them to avoid the racial sins of our past then the hope of racial harmony becomes all the more possible. It seems, though, that the "sins of
the fathers" have already been passed down even to toddlers.

If ever there was a reason for us to break the cycle of hatred that has
developed in our society, it is the future of our children. We must strive
to spare them the consequences of our sin. Yet our failure to do so is evi-

147

dent as this cycle of hate continues to play itself out. Turning a blind eye to the racial tensions that exist may temporarily assuage our feelings of guilt, but our children are not fooled and the end result of our sticking our head in the sand is our children's adoption of our tacit racist philosophies.

To be honest, this tendency to ignore problems of race belongs more to whites than to racial minorities. Minority parents may be guilty of allowing a racist ideology to go unchecked in their children or even of feeding that ideology, but rarely are such parents unaware of the importance that race plays in our country. This is because racial minorities have been forced to account for race most of their lives. We do not have the luxury of ignoring issues of race as whites do because such issues have touched us personally. All it takes is losing a job, a friendship, or an opportunity because of race. Since most of the positions of power are occupied by whites, I constantly have this issue of race on my mind as I move from encounter to encounter. A white person may suffer an occasional racist experience in his or her life, but race will probably never become a central issue of concern. This is because he or she will usually deal with other whites in power and not with racial minorities.

Once when I was in college, I was walking a good half a block behind a white woman. She glanced back at me and then suddenly and nervously hurried across the street away from me. Was this a natural reaction that she would have had to any male or was she reacting to the fact that I was black? That is a legitimate question because of the existence of racism in our country. African Americans can relate experiences of white women clutching their purses in elevators or whites locking their car doors as they drive through black neighborhoods. It is not unreasonable to assume that part of this reaction is due to a racial fear. Blacks must constantly deal with this kind of response. We cannot get away from race. We are reminded of its importance every time we interact with whites.

What I do with those reminders is the challenge that I and other racial minorities must face. Will we teach our children that we should seek an eye for an eye? Or will we adhere to Jesus' teaching and instruct our children in the art of forgiveness with lessons from the one who forgave us far more than we deserved? If we choose the latter action instead of the former, we can be part of the process of racial reconciliation.

Whites too must be part of the process of reconciliation. But often they must first take the painful step of acknowledging that severe racial problems exist. This may be painful as whites honestly look at the ways their race has oppressed minorities and how they themselves may have benefited from that oppression. If they pretend that a color-blind society exists today, they encourage the cycle of hatred to go on unabated, dooming their children to repeat the same mistakes.

It is important for whites to realize that, concerning race relations, there is no neutral ground. It is not just the problem of the other guys or a problem of the inner city. It is the problem of every American, and we must aggressively attack racist structures, challenging even subtle attitudes of bias that may creep into our thinking and the thinking of our peers.

Because our society is still influenced by racism, we will have to deliberately live an anti-racism lifestyle to teach others lessons of tolerance. Merely mouthing statements like "God created all of us equal" is not sufficient to compete with the dominance of racial stereotypes presented in the media or with the prevalence of racially biased attitudes heard every day. We must live out our commitment to equality, treating all people fairly, taking every opportunity to teach our children lessons of tolerance, and honestly assessing where our own biases may lie.

Living out the ideology of racial equality is more important than stating a belief in such a philosophy. If you forbid your son or daughter to date a racial minority, you have no further legitimacy in expressing an attitude of tolerance to your child. Your child will see your hypocrisy. However, working out the racial fears you may possess and allowing your child to be part of that process may prove to be a healing and growing experience for both of you.

It is only when we recognize the prevalence of racism and are willing to confront it that we will be able to break the cycle of hate. Of course we can't instantly change all of the factors that have contributed to racial injustices in America. Institutions such as the media, the courts, and the education system are not going to change merely because we have become aware of the problems intrinsic to them, and it is from institutions like these that our next generation learns to accept the racism of this generation. But there will be hope for change when enough of us in America come together to challenge the injustices coming out of these institutions. When we intentionally challenge racism, instead of ignoring it and hoping that it will go away, we may be able to extinguish even subtle manifestations of it.

Victims and Villains

You've got to be taught to hate and fear. . . .
You've got to be taught to be afraid
Of people whose eyes are oddly made
And people whose skin is a different shade.
You've got to be carefully taught.

Rodgers and Hammerstein
South Pacific

The truth behind this song was driven home to me on a camping trip. We took some young boys rock climbing. Instantly two fifth graders hit it off. One was white and the other black. As I watched their friendship grow, I realized that neither one of them seemed to realize that the other had a different skin color. They did not realize that society expects them to be uncomfortable with each other, to distrust each other, and to lack an ability to relate to each other's experience. They did not realize that they were supposed to stick to their own kind. No, they just had fun and played together the entire weekend. They reminded me that racism is truly a societal creation. We have no good reason for mistrusting individuals with different skin color or facial structure, and no sound rationale for segregation of such individuals. We merely continue to do so out of ignorance and insensitivity.

This forces me to wonder *Who did this to us?* Who said that it is all right for blacks to be bitter toward whites? Who said that it is fine for whites to discount the concerns of blacks? Who is the villain here? We Americans tend to think in terms of villains and victims. I want to know, Who is the villain in this situation?

I guess as a black man it is natural to point my finger at whites as the villains. After all, it is whites who brought my ancestors here against their will to enslave them. They have kept blacks down, using overt and subtle methods to ensure their power in this society. Many still refuse to acknowledge the advantage that they have gained by living in this society and instead concentrate their concerns on how unfair are the few gains that African Americans have made. Yes, as a black man I should say that it is the whites who are the villains.

Of course this leads to the conclusion that it is the minorities who are the victims of this situation. For all the same reasons that I could say whites are villains, I could also say minorities are victims. We have been forced to endure the oppression that whites have forced on us. We clearly do not deserve this injustice. So I could easily conclude that minorities are the victims.

Majority Victims

This is the typical way that racism is viewed in America—whites as villains and minorities as victims. There is a great deal of truth here, and much of this book has been devoted to revealing this relationship. But is this not a shortsighted view of what racism has done to our society? Can it be possible that whites might be victims as well? How many friendships have white Americans lost because of racial pressure and tensions? How many times have we seen a white American eaten up with racial hatred and unable to function well in our changing world? What about white Americans who desire to love others but cannot get over childhood lessons of prejudice and thus live with the guilt of irrational anger? What about the cost that fear of other races brings to white Americans?—a fear that must be maintained to keep the system of racial mistrust in place. Perhaps the ugliest part of the sin of racism is that those who seem to benefit the most from it, white Americans, really are having their souls corrupted and their lives spoiled by the soot and garbage that racism brings.

Many times the racial fears of white Americans entrap them. The only freedom they enjoy is in the realm of economic prosperity. This is not the freedom that the Bible promises. It talks about a freedom to do that which is right and to live out one's life to the fullest extent without being confined by the weaknesses of sin. Racism lies to whites by implying that they are free when in fact they are enslaved by their own fears and hatreds.

Sin has a way of seeming to offer us freedom even while it enslaves us. This aspect of sin is not limited to racism. When I was an impoverished

151

graduate student, I periodically sold my body to science. I participated in drug studies and often stayed at a facility for short periods of time. The pay for participating depended on whether or not I stayed until the study was complete.

Once while doing one of these studies I was cooped up with a group of men. One of them was driving the rest of us crazy. He was one of those goofy individuals who always wanted to be the center of attention. He used to put his finger in his mouth and stick it in our ears when we weren't looking. This was irritating to say the least.

For this study we came in on consecutive weekends. During the second to the last weekend the irritating man began to try to persuade the other members of the study to sneak out of the facility and go to a nightclub. At first I figured that no one would take him seriously. After all, if they were caught, they would forfeit the majority of their pay. However, to my surprise many of the men began to plan along with him on how they could sneak out the following weekend. Why would they listen to a man for whom they had very little respect? Why would they risk losing money to go out and party with someone whom they hated to be around?

This baffled me for a while, but then I realized that they were enslaved to this man. It was a slavery of their own choosing. They were not men of integrity—men who kept their word. Their lack of integrity made them vulnerable to whomever could push the right buttons and could manipulate their lack of honesty, even if they had no respect for that person.

Just as individuals who lack integrity often find themselves without the strength to do what they know is right, racists lack the ability to love people different from themselves even though they know their hatred is wrong. Freedom to hate often becomes slavery to hate. The perverted nature of sin, whether it is racism or lack of integrity, will often lead us down paths that we would rather not follow.

Many times whites have actively worked against racial equality or ignored the cries of injustice by their minority brothers and sisters thinking that in doing so they were furthering their own cause and the cause of their race. In reality they were also allowing their spirit to be soiled by hatred and letting this hatred dictate their actions. Actions of cruelty not only demean the individuals that endure those acts but also dehumanize the individuals who commit those acts. Individuals become monsters instead of men. They enjoy a false freedom that fools them into thinking that they are free to act as they want to act, but it is the freedom of an addict. It may give some whites the illusion of power and mastery, but all the while the addiction to hatred controls every action and feeling. So, too, can the drug of racism control all of our perceptions and force us into actions that we would normally be loath to take.

This is all too obvious when we are dealing with an overt racist; however, the overt racists are less numerous than the aversive racists. At least the overt racist realizes that racism can dominate his or her life. The aversive racist often fails to recognize the extent to which racism plays a role in his or her life. This individual suffers many of the same bondages that the overt racist suffers but at a lower level. Thus the aversive racist is enslaved by invisible chains. The aversive racist has lost his freedom to do what is right and does not even know that his freedom has been taken away. It is hard to imagine a more pitiful situation than for one to be a slave without even realizing it.

It is a lesson that we need to learn as a Christian body so that we can deal effectively with the problem of racism. We too often choose the short-term patterns that have been so successful for us in the past. I believe that deep down inside, we know that resisting racial diversity will be detrimental to us and our family in the long run. In the short run it seems to give us the illusion of control that we want. We choose the temporary taste of racial power even though it causes us to suffer the long-term illness of racial hatred. Since whites have the predominant place in this society, the temptation to enter this prison is even stronger for them than it is for blacks, even though blacks also can and do get caught up in the game of racial posturing for power. As long as racism retains its power in this country, white Americans will continue to fall for its hateful lies and will wind up trapped by its alluring temptation. They will lose their humanity and their compassion for other human beings. They will gain the world but lose their soul (see Matthew 16:26).

Racism is a truly ugly master that still holds many of our fellow brothers and sisters captive. Read these words from a noted Christian author:

> It took years for God to break the stranglehold of blatant racism in me—I wonder if any of us gets free of its more subtle forms—and I now see this sin as one of the most poisonous, with perhaps the greatest societal effects.[1]

We can make no mistake about it. This sin has caused a great deal of damage in individuals of all races. Certainly white people have been harmed by its devastating effects, even if they don't see how they have been harmed or recognize the damage that has been done to their person.

The concept of the white man being the victim is not a new one. Martin Luther King Jr. perceived this reality as well. In fact he saw his efforts as not just attempts to free blacks from obvious external oppression but also to help whites relieve the inner demons that racism often brings to the soul. Fortunately his nonviolent method was often successful for this purpose:

> The real goal, King used to say, was not to defeat the white man. . . . The end is reconciliation; the end is redemption; the end is the creation of the beloved community. And that is what Martin Luther King Jr. finally set into motion, even in a diehard racist like me.[2]

It is not enough that we find ways to bring racial justice to deprived minorities; we must also develop mechanisms that bring this justice to members of the majority race as well.

Minority Villains

If whites can be victims then can minorities be villains? Whites have given minorities plenty of reasons to hate them. But when that hate blooms into a distrust that paints all whites as evil creatures, then reconciliation becomes impossible. Blacks are right when they point out that the history of our country reveals how whites have gained the upper hand. They are correct when they argue that whites hold the institutional power and thus can keep blacks from progressing. If we are fair we must recognize that many of these problems have been addressed politically. While there is still room for a further refinement of our political process, I am of the opinion that we have gone just about as far as we can with politics, unless what blacks want is more power instead of real equality. There must be a relationship developed between blacks and whites. This relationship cannot form unless blacks allow it to form.

A big part of the problem comes out of the philosophy of black power. This philosophy is founded on a nationalism that emphasizes the ability of blacks to take care of themselves apart from whites, as well as a need to be separated from a corrupting white influence. The development of this philosophy is a natural reaction to the abuse that most African Americans have suffered at the hand of the dominant culture. There are seeds

154

of truth here. African Americans do need to take control of their own lives and to recognize the disadvantages that they face in this society. However, when it comes to reconciliation, such a philosophy is unable to promote the building of relationships based on equality because it replaces white arrogance with black arrogance. It does not seek to build relationships but to completely sever relationships. The philosophy of black power victimizes whites because it denies whites the ability to build solid relationships with blacks.

I am convinced that the only permanent solution to racial injustice is reconciliation and relationship. Without relationship, black power only shifts the offended party from blacks to whites. Without reconciliation government programs tend to intensify alienation instead of acceptance. Unfortunately many of my black brothers and sisters are just as adamantly against reconciliation as the Ku Klux Klan. When minorities refuse to see whites as anything but potential villains, relationship becomes impossible. While I understand why many blacks are hesitant to trust whites, I also know that we can never kill racism in our society until we risk trusting others. As difficult as it is for minorities to realize this, we must recognize that when whites want a relationship and when minorities refuse to allow that relationship to develop, then it is the minorities who are the villains, allowing racial hatred to continue to flourish.

I have white friends who are honestly attempting to understand minorities and to build the bridges that are so desperately needed for us to overcome this hatred. Even when rebuffed, many of them continue to seek out relationships with minorities. While they should and must be patient, patience does have limits. At some point we have to allow some whites to know us. We must work to stop the hatred and teach our children to stop the hatred. If we don't, we blacks doom ourselves to fight against a white race that historically and institutionally retains the advantages and will win this struggle.

Racial reconciliation is the process by which we renegotiate a new relationship built on equality. In an equal relationship minorities can be villains as well as victims. It is part of the cost of equality. However, it is a cost that we should be happy to pay if it will end the antagonism the races now feel toward each other. As we come together and struggle to learn about each other, there will be painful lessons. Ultimately, however, we will learn that "the other" is not as strange as we may have

155

thought. We will learn to put away the fears and stereotypes that now inhibit us and will witness the development of true racial harmony.

Blacks and whites are both villains and victims. Somehow that feels right. Sin is never limited to a particular group. Eventually all groups involved in a conflict begin to sin against the other groups in that conflict. It is our nature to sin. When we remember this, then maybe we will not be so eager to find the villain in others. Maybe we can be honest, examine ourselves, and find the villain in us. Maybe we can also recognize that while we are victims, others are victims as well. If we do this, we may start to die to our own needs and become more concerned with the needs of others.

156

Where Integration
Must Happen

Racial integration . . . has produced the symbols of progress and the
rhetoric of racial harmony without the substance of empowerment
for the oppressed.

Manning Marable

We social scientists sometimes like to think of ourselves as fix-
ers of society. Sometimes attempts at social engineering end in disaster,
but often it is done with the best intentions in mind. The failure of social
scientists to correct what sometimes may seem like simple problems is a
testimony to the inadequacy of human ability.

Take racism for instance. You would think that it would be easy to teach
people that such a philosophy is unproductive. Why would you give up a
potential friend, ally, lover, or comrade simply because of the color of that
person's skin? Racism is a concept that makes no sense whatsoever.

For decades sociologists have studied the phenomenon of racism. For
decades measures have been in place with the purpose of eradicating
racism. How much success have we experienced? Unfortunately not
much. Multicultural programs designed to create an appreciation of other
cultures often instead serve to resegregate our campuses. Affirmative action
programs have failed to substantially increase the economic welfare and
opportunities of minorities. Civil Rights laws protect minorities from the
most overt acts of racism but are often unable to protect them from institutional and aversive racism.

The point isn't that we should never have tried these programs. Indeed,
the life of minorities might be worse today if these efforts had not been

157

made. But we still have a long way to go. It is important to recognize and analyze our failures so that we can learn from them and create new methods that may be successful.

Why have most of the traditional programs that attempt to fight racism failed? Why is it we can combat overt discrimination but seem unable to affect the prejudice that lies below the surface? Answers to these tough questions do not come easily. Perhaps Gaertner and Dovidio have stumbled on an answer through their example of how school desegregation has failed to reduce the hostile feelings between the races.[1] They observed that in desegregated schools the races tend to compete with each other and develop stronger hostile feelings toward each other rather than learning to understand and accept each other. This runs counter to the hypothesis that the more the different races intertact with each other, the more they will get along. Gaertner and Dovidio conclude that mere contact between the races is not enough for harmony to develop. The contact must be made within certain criteria.

> We suggest that superordinate goals successfully reduce intergroup conflict . . . because they increase the likelihood that members of these groups will perceive themselves as belonging to one group rather than two. . . . it is possible that intergroup cooperation not only reduces the salience of the intergroup boundary but also contributes to members' perceiving the existence of one entity rather than two.[2]

I know that initially this sounds like a bunch of intellectual gobbledygook, but underneath it may lie some answers to our questions. If Gaertner and Dovidio are correct, we may be able to assert two factors to be of importance if we want individuals to begin to look past racial boundaries. One, we must have an institution that encourages goals that encompass all the racial groups. Integrated schools fail to do this because success is individualized. With such individualized goals there is no need for different racial groups to work together. Second, there must be mechanisms that promote cooperation instead of competition. Once again, schools fail because competition for grades and honors remains the powerful motivator for many individuals.

If interracial contact within the schools cannot foster racial acceptance, then where can this contact be useful? It must be where there are goals that are greater than the individual goals of the people involved and where there is more incentive for cooperation than competition. This happens in the family. In the family individuals learn to subordinate their own personal goals for the greater good of the family. In families we learn the benefits of cooperation, and competition is often downplayed. In a healthy family children don't have to compete for their parents' love. They all receive it equally. The family then becomes a viable format through which racial healing can take place.

Perhaps this is one of the reasons why the concept of interracial marriages has intrigued me and I have done so much research on this topic. As part of an interracial family, one can easily learn the cost of racism and develop a distaste for it. One learns not merely to tolerate other races but to truly love them. Part of the solution to racial healing will be the creation of interracial families that will challenge the traditional barriers that racism has placed on us.

I know that this is not the complete answer. If we have to wait for families to become interracial before we can end the scourge of racism, we have a long wait indeed. But there is another institution where overarching goals and cooperation may serve to help end the racial division that has developed. That institution is the church. Those of us who profess Christ as Savior should look to him and his interest, rather than to any of our own individual racial interests. As his body we unite in the goals of serving and being obedient to him. As his body we have a common enemy, Satan, whom we must fight. To do this effectively there must be cooperation among us. Theoretically, then, the church should be an ideal place for the eradication of racism because it's a place of shared goals and cooperation.

Why then is Sunday morning the most segregated time of the week? Obviously it is because we in the church have allowed the same racist garbage of the world to be carried into our sanctuaries. In other words we have allowed sin to become commonplace in our churches. As long as this is the case, we can never expect to be an effective witness to our society on the issue of racism, much less provide the solution (even though it's ours to give).

If the solution is to come from the church, we must get our own house in order. The church must begin to make an overt and conscious effort to further the integration process so that one day our nation will be healed of this sickness. It will not happen by accident. This effort must be deliberate. There must be repentance that may be painful. There must be forgiveness that will seldom be easy to give.

The racism of the past has brought us to our present situation. We can neither ignore it nor dwell in it. We as Christians must chart the future, preparing ourselves for the harmony that God means for us to have.

My secular friends are still looking for the way to fix the seemingly intractable problem of racism. They do not share my conviction that the church is the only place where racism can be effectively dealt with. They have good reason to be skeptical of my faith in the church. They, as well as I, know that often the church has intensified racial hatred instead of alleviating it. Christian doctrine has often been used to justify supremacist beliefs and slavery. Unfortunately Christians have often been quiet while racial atrocities took place all around them. Many times it has been the irreligious who have fought for racial equality. In the light of all of this failure, it's no surprise that people doubt the ability of the church to offer the solution.

If we were relying only on the goodwill of Christians, my friends are probably right. Some of the most hateful racial dogma that I have heard has come from individuals who claim to be Christians. More than once I have felt racial rejection from individuals who are thought to be followers of Christ. As humans we Christians are often no better than the non–Christians that we sometimes look down on.

Yet I think about Gaertner and Dovidio's study and the requirements an institution needs to have to deal with racism. And I recognize that, other than the family, there is no other organization that seems to meet these criteria. It is then that I recognize that the success or failure of the church is not dependent on us weak Christians but on the powerful Lord who has designed his church for such a time. I believe he has appointed us to do what the rest of society is unable to do. We know that it is not our strength that is important but the strength of the Lord who sustains us. There is too much in our history that works against our trusting each other. We must trust him so that we can learn how to love each other. Even though I am often at a loss as to what the particular answers to different racial problems may be, I know that it must be in the church, not the secular world, where the solutions ultimately lie. I am convinced that when our determination to obey the Lord is higher than our desire to gain power and ease for ourselves, we in the body of Christ will be able to offer the world answers to the problem of racism.

Will you be part of this mighty solution? Do you want to participate in this powerful witness? It will not be easy. In fact it will be more than we can manage in our own power. But that's good. Because that means we have to rely on God all the more, for he can deliver us from this racial infirmity. In him we can truly be one.

Epilogue

What a Waste!

> If one member suffers, all the members suffer with it; if one member is honored, all the members rejoice with it.
>
> 1 Corinthians 12:26

I want to end this book by telling you about my grandfather. Even though I spent much of my childhood in the classic single-parent household, I was saved from gang involvement and crime by the influence of my grandfather when I was a teenager. In fact I lived with my grandparents during my high school years. Other than the Lord, and possibly my mother, I believe that the person who is the most responsible for my obtaining an education is my grandfather.

Most boys want to imitate their fathers. I strove to imitate my grandfather. He had a laid-back personality that enabled him to withstand the trials of life easier than most people. But that laid-back personality did not keep him from speaking his mind if he felt strongly about an issue. I have tried to adopt these qualities. My grandfather also had a wonderful childlike part to his personality, from which came his sense of humor. Once when he found us playing tackle football with some girls down the street (you can probably guess our motivations for this game), I thought I was in trouble, but his natural response was "Can I play too?"

I most admired my grandfather's wisdom. Despite all the intelligent people that I have met in academia and in the church, I have still not found anyone who has the wisdom of my grandfather. No one I have known has done more with less opportunity than my grandfather. As a teacher of what life is all about, I could not find a better instructor. The loss of his wisdom at his death deeply touched my life.

But in addition to wisdom, he was also an incredible man of book knowledge. From his influence on me, I developed a healthy respect for knowledge and a resolve to pursue a higher education. I wish I could say that I am as intelligent as my grandfather. The truth of the matter is that I am not even close.

My grandfather's expertise was in electronics. He spent his life collecting and mastering different electronic equipment that I still do not understand. I often went into his workroom and imagined that I was in one of those elaborate laboratories that we so often see in science fiction films. When Grandfather died my grandmother wanted to give this equipment to a local college, but most of it was too sophisticated for the college to use.

I remember my grandfather building a computer. Now, my grandfather's computer would not hold a candle to the powerful instrument that I am typing this story on. It looked like a small version of one of those monster computers that are run by huge tape reels—computers that were around before microchips and microcircuits. In the late 1960s, long before the terms RAM and ROM were commonplace, my grandfather built his computer. I was a child at the time and too young to know all that this computer could do. It was rather crude but it worked! It would be an accomplishment today for a man to build a computer from scratch. To do so in the late 1960s only reveals the depths of the intellectual abilities of my grandfather.

To fully appreciate these accomplishments one must realize that my grandfather never received a college education. All of the knowledge he ever gained about electronics he gained on his own by reading books and doing his own experiments. As a young man, my grandfather simply did not have the option of going to college, so he went into the Air Force and spent most of his life there. The military was one of the few places where a black man could make small but real gains in life. Under the occupational security of the military service my grandfather was free to pursue his interests in electronics. Eventually his expertise with electronics caught the attention of his supervisors in the Air Force. Toward the end of his service he worked on sensitive electronic equipment in some of the aircraft, even though he never rose past the rank of master sergeant and never took a college class.

Very few people know who George M. Yancey was. I wonder what might have happened if my grandfather had gone to college and had been able to develop his abilities to their fullest extent. Of course no one can know for certain, but doesn't it seem likely that a man with the natural ability that he possessed would have made tremendous contributions to the electronics industry? If his talents had been recognized earlier, he might have done more than build a crude computer or tinker with electronics on aircraft. He might have invented the next generation of personal computers or furthered the research program of a major institution. We will never know all that my grandfather was capable of accomplishing, and I believe it is fair to say that it was our society that robbed him of the opportunities to develop his talents to their fullest extent and to collect a fair reward for those talents.

My grandfather is not the only one who was robbed. His whole family would have benefited from his accomplishments. My family might have had the material resources that would have made our lives easier. While never poor, my grandparents did not have the money to put my mother or aunt through college. When it came time for me to go on to school there was not money for my schooling either. I did not think much of it at the time, but now I wonder how much easier it would have been if my family could have at least paid my tuition, freeing me to concentrate on my studies instead of a job. How much better could my mother have prepared me for the expectations that college would demand if she had gone as a young woman. When one multiplies this effect by my three brothers one finds a multitude of lives that were affected by the denial of my grandfather's ability to exercise his gifts.

But I am being selfish, because in truth the entire society has suffered from the loss of the contributions my grandfather could have made. If he could have developed a new generation of computers, just think that you could probably now have an updated version of your current computer at the same price you paid for it. If he had invented some improved communication system, perhaps car phones would be cheaper and more accessible today. He might have invented a new kind of hearing aid or television, any number of things. Now, I realize that this is just speculation. It's possible that my grandfather, even with the opportunities afforded many young white Americans, would not have created some invention that would have dramatically affected our lives today. But we will never know. He had no money to go to college; he had no family tradition of college attendance to encourage him; he had no scholarship offers; he had no good job offers with promises of promotion, and so, for the most part, his talents lay dormant. In a real way, because he was black, our society cheated him of opportunities to realize his potential.

When you think about a life like my grandfather's you begin to realize what a waste racism truly is. The overt racism suffered by my grandfather robbed all of us of his ability to serve us. In a time like today when we are in an economic battle with Europe and Japan, we simply do not have any resources to waste because of foolish racial barriers. We must give every individual a complete chance of success in our society so that we can all enjoy the fruits of that success. Truly what harms one will harm everyone. To this end, all of us must be on our guard to make sure that no more George M. Yanceys live and die without giving society everything that they have to give.

Racism is an irrational system that does not even benefit those who enforce it. On a personal level it robs an individual of the ability to be fully human and to completely enjoy all the wonders that life has to offer. On a societal level racism deprives us of all of the talents that this nation needs to compete in our global economy. It creates two victims instead of one and traps them in a cycle of hatred. Such a system deeply deserves the death that we Christians must hasten to give it.

Notes

Chapter 2 We Made It Up

1. General Social Survey (Chicago: National Opinion Research Center, 1994). Roughly 20 percent of all whites polled believed that there should be a law to forbid interracial marriages.

Chapter 3 Real Racism or Guilt Trip?

1. Shelby Steele, *The Content of Our Character: A New Vision of Race in America* (New York: St. Martin's Press, 1990), 240.

2. Ibid., 4–6.

3. Ibid.

4. Ibid., 138.

Chapter 4 Modern Racism

1. John B. McConahay, "Modern Racism, Ambivalence, and the Modern Racism Scale," in *Prejudice, Discrimination, and Racism,* ed. John F. Dovidio and Samuel L. Gaertner (Orlando: Academic Press, 1986).

2. *Statistical Abstract of the United States, 1991* (Washington, D.C.: U.S. Government Printing Office).

3. *The Black Population in the United States: March 1990 and 1989,* series P-20, no. 448 (Washington, D.C.: U.S. Government Printing Office, 1991).

4. Bureau of Labor Statistics, *Employment in Perspective: Minority Workers, Fourth Quarter* (Washington, D.C.: U.S. Government Printing Office, 1991).

Chapter 5 Why?

1. Perhaps even more interesting is the fact that some in the academic community have begun to recognize this bias. The best example of this is Stephen Warner, "Theoretical Barriers to the Understanding of Evangelical Christianity," *Sociological Analysis* 40, no. 1 (1979): 1–9. He argues that the politically liberal tendencies of sociologists gear them to see evangelical Christians in a negative light due to the social conservatism they see within Christianity.

Chapter 6 Can a Black Be Racist?

1. See, for example, Frank Minirth and Paul Meier, *Happiness Is a Choice: A Manual on the Symptoms, Causes, and Cures of Depression* (Grand Rapids: Baker, 1978).

Chapter 7 I'm Not Racist but . . .

1. Tony Evans, *Let's Get to Know Each Other: What White Christians Should Know about Black Christians* (Nashville: Thomas Nelson, 1994), 135–38.

Chapter 8 Institutional Discrimination

1. Andrew Hacker, *Two Nations: Black and White, Separate, Hostile, Unequal* (New York: Ballantine Books, 1992), 36.

2. Ronald Sider, *Rich Christians in an Age of Hunger: A Biblical Study* (Downers Grove, Ill.: InterVarsity Press, 1978), 132–33.

3. There are two studies that confirm this observation: Farley Reynolds, Suzanne Bianchi, and Diane Colasanto, "Barriers to the Racial Integration of Neighborhoods: The Detroit Case," *The Annals of the American Academy of Political and Social Science* 441 (January 1979): 97–113; and Farley Reynolds, Suzanne Bianchi, Diane Colasanto, and Shirley Hatchett, "Chocolate City, Vanilla Suburbs: Will the Trend Towards Racially Separated Communities Continue?" *Social Science Research* 7 (1978): 319–44. In these studies both whites and blacks were asked hypothetically whether they would be willing to move to neighborhoods of varying degrees of racial integration. While 85 percent of the blacks were willing to live in a neighborhood that was half white and half black, only about a quarter of the whites were willing to live in such a neighborhood.

Chapter 9 The Requirements of Discrimination

1. According to information given on *Prime Time Live*'s 1992 Thanksgiving program "True Colors," African Americans pay on the average $1,010 more for a car than do whites.

2. One example is found in Christopher G. Ellison, "Religious Involvement and Self-Perception among Black Americans," *Social Forces* 71, no. 4 (June 1993): 1027–56. He examines the concept of personal mastery, which is similar to self-efficacy. He finds that while the self-esteem of African Americans does not differ from that of whites, personal mastery is lower than it is for whites.

Chapter 14 Finger Pointing

1. Steele, *The Content of Our Character*, 93–109.

Chapter 15 A Book by Its Cover

1. S. Steenland, "The Unequal Picture: Black, Hispanic, Asian and Native American Characters on Television," *Hartford Courant*, 26 August 1989, B2.

2. James Bayton, "The Racial Stereotype of Negro College Students," *The Journal of Abnormal and Social Psychology* 36 (1941): 97–102.

3. Kenneth Clark and Mamie Clark, "Racial Identification and Preference in Negro Children," in Society for the Study of Social Issues, *Readings in Social Psychology* (New York: Henry Holt, 1947), 169–78.

4. D. Powell-Hopson and D. S. Hopson, "Implications of Doll Color Preferences among Black Preschool Children and White Preschool Children," *Journal of Black Psychology* 14, no. 2 (1988): 57–63.

Chapter 19 Acceptance at the Most Intimate Level

1. Jeanette R. Davidson, "Black–White Interracial Marriage: A Critical Look at Theories about Motivations of the Partners," *Journal of Intergroup Relations* 14 (winter 1991–92): 14–20.

2. Walter Wangerin, "The Education of Matthew Wangerin," *Christianity Today* 35 (May 1991): 16–19.

3. Gordon Allport, *The Nature of Prejudice* (Garden City, N.Y.: Doubleday, 1958), 23.

Chapter 20 The Bible and Interracial Marriage

1. "Bob Jones University: Doing Battle in the Name of Religion and Freedom," *Change* 15 (May/June 1983): 38–47.

2. Examples of these statements can be found in Nehemiah 13:23–25; Deuteronomy 7:3; and 1 Kings 11:1–2.

3. See Exodus 34:14–16; Nehemiah 13:26; Deuteronomy 7:3–4; and 1 Kings 11:4.

Chapter 21 What about the Children?

1. Christine C. Iijima Hall, "The Ethnic Identity of Racially Mixed People: A Study of Black Japanese" (Ph.D. diss., UCLA, 1980); George Kitahara Kich, "Eurasians: Ethnic/Racial Identity Development of Biracial Japanese/White Adults" (Ph.D. diss., Wright Institute, Berkeley, Calif., 1982); and Francis Wilson, "Are You Sensitive to Interracial Children's Special Identity Needs?" *Young Children* (January 1987), 53–58.

2. Walter Stephan and Cookie Stephan, "Intermarriage: Effects on Personality, Adjustment and Intergroup Relations in Two Samples of Students," *Journal of Marriage and the Family* 53 (February 1991): 241–50.

3. C. McKinley, "Custody Disputes Following the Dissolution of Interracial Marriages: Best Interest of the Child or Judicial Racism?" *Journal of Family Law* 19, no. 1 (1981): 97–136.

Chapter 22 Can Christianity and Racism Mix?

1. Richard J. Herrnstein and Charles Murray, *The Bell Curve: Intelligence and Class Structure in American Life* (New York: The Free Press, 1994).

2. Keith Roberts, *Religion in Sociological Perspective* (Homewood, Ill.: The Dorsey Press, 1984), 331.

3. Martin Luther King Jr., *Strength to Love* (New York: Harper and Row, 1963), 136.

Chapter 24 Beyond Black and White

1. There are many studies that document these and other similar findings. Some of them are Joan Petersilia, *Racial Disparities in the Criminal Justice System* (Santa Monica, Calif.: Rand, 1983); David Huizinga and Delbert S. Elliott, "Juvenile Offenders: Prevalence, Offender Incidence, and Arrest Rates by Race," *Crime and Delinquency* 33 (April 1987): 206–23; George S. Bridges and Robert D. Crutchfield, "Law, Social Standing and Racial Disparities in Imprisonment," *Social Forces* 66 (March 1988): 699–724; and Stephen P. Klein, Susan Turner, and Joan Petersilia, *Racial Equity in Sentencing* (Santa Monica, Calif.: Rand, 1988).

2. David C. Baldus, Charles Pulaski, and George Woodworth, "Comparative Review of Death Sentences: An Empirical Study of the Georgia Experience," *The Journal of Criminal Law and Criminology* 74 (1983): 661–73; Samuel R. Gross and Robert Mauro, *Death and Discrimination: Racial Disparities in Capital Sentencing* (Boston: Northeastern University Press, 1989).

Chapter 26 Talk Shows, Jobs, and Interracial Dating

1. Studs Terkel, *Race: How Blacks and Whites Think and Feel about the American Obsession* (New York: The New Press, 1992), 5.

2. Gunnar Myrdal, *An American Dilemma* (New York: Harper and Brothers, 1944), 60–61.

3. Milton M. Gordon, *Assimilation in American Life* (New York: Oxford, 1964).

Chapter 27 One in Christ

1. Frank Westie, "The American Dilemma: An Empirical Test," *American Sociological Review* 30 (August 1965): 531–32.

Chapter 28 Living in Sin

1. Robert Merton, "Discrimination and the American Creed," in Norman Yetman, ed., *Majority and Minority: The Dynamics of Race and Ethnicity in American Life* (Boston: Allyn and Bacon, 1985), 40–53.

2. George Kelsey, *Racism and the Christian Understanding of Man* (New York: Scribner, 1965).

Chapter 29 Breaking the Cycles of Hate

1. Debra Van Ausdale, "Race and Ethnicity in the Everyday Interactions of Very Young Children" (paper presented at the annual meeting of the American Sociological Association, Los Angeles, Calif., August 5–10, 1994).

Chapter 30 Victims and Villains

1. Phillip Yancey, "Confessions of a Racist: It Wasn't Until after Martin Luther King Jr.'s Death That I Was Struck by the Truth of What He Lived and Preached," *Christianity Today* 34, no. 1 (15 January 1990), 26.

2. Ibid.

Chapter 31 Where Integration Must Happen

1. Samuel L. Gaertner and John F. Dovidio, "Prejudice, Discrimination, and Racism: Problems, Progress, and Promise," in *Prejudice, Discrimination, and Racism,* ed. Dovidio and Gaertner, 318–19.

2. Ibid., 323–25.

Bibliography

Cleaver, Eldridge. *Soul on Ice*. New York: Dell, 1968.

Colson, Charles. *Loving God*. Grand Rapids: Zondervan, 1987.

————. *Who Speaks for God? Confronting the World with Real Christianity*. Westchester, Ill.: Crossway Books, 1985.

Evans, Tony. *Let's Get to Know Each Other: What White Christians Should Know about Black Christians*. Nashville: Thomas Nelson, 1994.

Feagin, Joe. *Racial and Ethnic Relations*. 2nd ed. Englewood Cliffs, N.J.: Prentice-Hall, 1984.

Grant, Madison. *The Passing of the Great Race*. New York: Scribner, 1916.

Hacker, Andrew. *Two Nations: Black and White, Separate, Hostile, Unequal*. New York: Ballantine, 1992.

King, Martin Luther, Jr. *Strength to Love*. New York: Harper and Row, 1963.

————. *Why We Can't Wait*. New York: Penguin, 1964.

Malcolm X. *The Autobiography of Malcolm X*. New York: Ballantine, 1965.

Marable, Manning. "The Rhetoric of Racial Harmony." *Sojourners* (August / September 1990): 15–19.

Pannell, William. *The Coming Race Wars? A Cry for Reconciliation*. Grand Rapids: Zondervan, 1993.

Paton, Alan. *Cry, the Beloved Country*. New York: Macmillan, 1987.

Perkins, Spencer, and Chris Rice. *More than Equals: Racial Healing for the Sake of the Gospel*. Downers Grove, Ill.: InterVarsity, 1993.

Sider, Ronald. *Rich Christians in an Age of Hunger: A Biblical Study*. Downers Grove, Ill.: InterVarsity, 1978.

Sister Souljah. "Rap and Race." *Newsweek* 66, no. 26 (June 29, 1992): 48.

Solzhenitsyn, Alexandr I. *The Gulag Archipelago 1918–1956,* trans. Thomas P. Whitney. New York: Harper and Row, 1975.

Steele, Shelby. *The Content of Our Character: A New Vision of Race in America*. New York: St. Martin's Press, 1990.

George A. Yancey is visiting assistant professor of sociology in the Division of Social and Policy Sciences at the University of Texas at San Antonio. He received his Ph.D. from the University of Texas at Austin.